Confessions of a
Female Safety Engineer

Confessions of a
Female Safety Engineer

Wendy S. Delmater

Abyss & Apex Publishing, LLC

Confessions of a Female Safety Engineer
Copyright © 2017 by Wendy S. Delmater

ISBN 13: 978-1975987770
ISBN-10: 1975987772

Cover art © Jeff Lee Johnson
Cover design by Wendy S. Delmater
Formatting by Susan H. Roddey

Published by: Abyss & Apex Publishing, LLC
Attention: Wendy S. Delmater
116 Tennyson Drive
Lexington, SC 29073
USA

www.abyssapexzine.com
abyssandapex@gmail.com

Printed by CreateSpace

CONTENTS

CONTENTS (cont'd.)

"Safety guidelines are written in blood."

–safety truism

The Engineer's Dilemma

It's not my place to run the train
The whistle I can't blow.
It's not my place to say how far
The train's allowed to go.
It's not my place to shoot off steam
Nor even clang the bell.
But let the damn thing jump the track
And see who catches hell!
–author unknown

Dedicated to safety managers the world over,
and especially women in the safety field.
You are the ones who make sure workers go home in one piece at night.
Thank You.

Acknowledgements

Thank you to my beta readers: Alexander Pournelle and Brian Thies. Alex, in particular, asked probing questions that rounded out the book and made it more engaging. Tom Simon and Tonya Liburd also both proofread the book and cheered me on while writing it.

Thank you to Susan Roddey for your interior book design work, and to Jeff Lee Johnson for your (as usual) amazing cover art.

Special thanks are due to my friend Lucy A. Snyder's followers on Facebook. I would not have realized that anyone wanted to hear these stories until they insisted they wanted them told.

And a heartfelt thank you to all of the dedicated people who work tirelessly to keep our workplaces safe and secure. You are truly some of the unsung heroes and heroines of our modern age.

AUTHOR'S NOTE

I SPENT MY LAST COUPLE OF DECADES BETWEEN WORLDS. CONSTRUCTION safety management is "gray collar" work; that means it bridges the gap between white collar professionals and blue collar labor. By and large, my career was all about translating from one world to another.

I've also spent the last few decades translating thoughts, writing and editing. I've spent two years as the national newsletter editor for the construction division of the American Society of Safety Engineers, edited an online science fiction magazine (Abyss & Apex) that is known for finding new talent, written books on how to find a spouse in midlife, and I've written a volume that tries to explain the experience of depression to the non-depressed. These creative projects were also all about explaining one world to another.

Welcome to my world.

Confessions of a Female Safety Engineer is an inside look at hidden New York. Construction in New York City is divorced from the overall culture of the metropolis, which only intrudes when a tradesman plays music on his radio or they talk about sports scores. And within the world of construction management, there is no odder place to be than that of the construction safety engineer.

I will also take you inside obscure neighborhoods and introduces you to unforgettable characters. The stories are true, although many of the names have been changed to protect the innocent, or the absurd.

Come along on an adventure I never expected, where a woman gets to participate in one of the last bastions of work in a male-dominated field. These are my field notes from the other side.

It's been a hell of a ride.

Wendy S. Delmater

How I Got Into This - or - "I'd Rather Be Baking Cookies."

I WAS ABANDONED WITH THREE SMALL SONS, AGED SIX (DAN), FIVE (CHRIS), and three (Jon), to provide for. At the time my ex-husband was not paying anything toward the children. And when he did eventually pay child support, it was only $100 a week for all three of our kids. So, I had to work outside the home. And as I looked around me I saw a disturbing trend: single mothers who worked two jobs in the "Pink Collar Ghetto" to make ends meet. Maybe they'd work as house or office cleaners on top of being waitresses or home health aides or clerks. This meant they were never home and their children in effect lost both parents. I did not want my sons to lose me as a parent, too.

I therefore looked for a single high-paying job to support us, one job only, so I would have time to be a parent. And I found that high pay rates ultimately meant either an advanced degree which I did not have time for, or looking at non-traditional work for women in male-dominated fields.

But which field? I was determined that my work be something I could at least be good at and enjoy, because I'd seen first-hand while growing up how doing work you hated could sap your strength and steal your soul. My father had been a Navy pilot in WWII: carrier landings, flying inside of hurricanes, the works. He loved to fly, lived for it. Then his eyes went on him, back when you could not wear glasses and fly. So he got an honorable discharge, and went to college on the GI Bill. He opted for a 'safe' tenured teaching career. And although he was very good at teaching, he hated it. His heart was in the sky, and my father became a bitter six-pack-a-night alcoholic who sat there and watched old war movies when not taking out his frustrations on his family.

I was determined to take a lesson from that. So yes, I was looking for a high-paying, traditionally male position, but it had to be something I liked. I was also looking for a career in a field that would not be taken over by automation or shipped overseas. And I had to be able to take my existing experience as a restaurant manager and the person who ran my ex's home improvement

1

business office, and be able to start making decent money before our foreclosed house was taken by the bank.

Luckily for me I was offered free occupational counseling and testing by a local charity. The testing told me that I worked well alone, and should avoid things I was not constitutionally suited for, like accountancy. I learned my various marketable traits. They suggested I get a copy of *What Color is Your Parachute*[ii], so I did. The triangulation exercises in that book helped me map paths from where I was to where I wanted to be. I could not go back into restaurant management since that would mean I only worked when the kids were not in school but...management. One thing stood out in those exercises; my management skills were transferrable.

While I contemplated a new career I worked as an office temp. I also learned the ropes of being truly poor, navigating various government agencies and learning the brutal facts about how our system has failed them. Because I was living rent-free in a foreclosed home and made $6 an hour I only qualified for assistance with childcare costs! My sons and I made do with thrift store clothes and food bank food. Thanks to my brother sending me old computers with software installed, I learned at home how to type and use a PC, and I got familiar with various programs that would help me earn a living: MS-Word, Excel, PowerPoint, and some desktop publishing.

As an office temp I could see a trend from the inside: in the late 80s companies gave secretaries a little more money and called them "administrative assistants" when they learned programs like Excel, and then the companies used the admins plus a spreadsheet program to replace most of expensive middle management. Otherwise, managers did their own administrative work. So if I went into management I would probably never have a secretary; I'd be lucky to share an admin. I'd need to learn the software skills I was honing as a temp to survive in management.

I also noted an unexpected pattern. Let's call it "Wendy's High School Lunch Table Theory." The same like-minded folks that hung out together in high school seemed to congregate at the same businesses. In high school there were the jocks, the artsy types, the fashion plates, the mean girls, the geeks... and now as an office temporary I discovered that there were offices that seemed to attract similar personality types. Like my father teaching, I might do well at a business full of very different people than me, but I'd not be comfortable.

2

Still, no matter where they placed me, as an office temp I learned quickly. I picked up positions like Executive Secretary and doing monster spreadsheets for huge companies. And then a temp agency placed me at the job that would change my life forever.

SCARCITY IS YOUR FRIEND

AS AN OFFICE TEMP I NOT ONLY LEARNED SCARCE SKILLS, MOSTLY IN EXCEL since I was not a fast typist, but once I had those spreadsheet skills I quickly learned how to play the temp agencies against each other. I was registered with multiple agencies—temp-to-perm ones that tended to have longer assignments—and when one temp firm had no work the others always did. When multiple agencies offered me temp positions I'd take the higher-paying one.

One of the three agencies I was registered with saw my experience running my ex's home improvement company's office for ten years and placed me at a large construction site startup, as a combination admin and plan clerk to the general contractor until they could get an admin who was a faster typist. The first week I was stuck in an office trailer that had no heat in February since the electricity was not hooked up yet. We worked in parkas wearing fingerless gloves, by daylight. As someone who loved to go camping it was rather fun, actually. And the people were great: hard working, dedicated, witty, and smart. This was an office environment that attracted people from a "lunch table" I'd be comfortable at. Bonus! The job was during school hours for my kids, and five minutes from home.

In a few weeks the construction office moved into a nearby building, an abandoned mental hospital office, slogan, "You don't have to be crazy to work here but it helps." In a few more weeks a fellow came from their corporate office to do safety orientations for the staff and each subcontractor as the trades were signed on. This was a revelation to me. The only thing I'd enjoyed about being a restaurant manager was the safety work. You mean, I could do safety full time?

I checked out the possibility of doing safety management as a career. It paid well. More importantly, the work was not considered an overhead expense as it paid for itself with employers in lowered Worker Compensation insurance costs and lower litigation costs. Furthermore, this work was in no danger of being replaced by technology or being shipped overseas. I found that there was a huge need for safety managers. And what was even better was that hardly anyone wanted to do it!

By this time the construction company had hired me away from the temp agency. From the instant I told them I wanted to do construction safety work, full time, their corporate safety office did all they could to get me into that position. It seemed that they were constantly training people to be safety managers and losing them; project managers and superintendents wanted to "get a little safety on their resume" and would go back to being PMs and supers after being trained. The fact that I wanted to do safety, and *only* safety, really appealed to them.

The construction company immediately had me meet with their corporate safety manager, who signed me up to take an associates-degree-equivalent correspondence course with *The Alliance of American Insurers*. The safety director put my training under the auspices of the site project engineer. I was given the title Assistant Safety Manager and pursued my studies while simultaneously handling the plan clerk work for a $178-million dollar project.

At this point, I got back out my copy of *What Color is Your Parachute*[iii] and did the triangulation exercises again. This time I had a more definite goal in mind. What would be my path to being a safety manager? There were several.

My research told me that safety management jobs branched into three paths: Insurance, Industrial, and Construction. Construction safety managers had the highest pay, the biggest labor shortage, and the most payoff for the companies they worked for since the workers they managed were considered high-risk by insurers, and a safe track record in construction meant a company paid *substantially* less in insurance.

Construction safety management itself had two main paths: one could follow large construction companies around the USA and the world (and hope to not get laid off and abandoned in a strange place), or one could base oneself in a major metropolitan area and do various construction projects there. As I did not want to drag my small children around the country, and lived near New York City, I chose what seemed to be the most stable of the two options, a location-based construction safety management career. So how would that work in NYC?

Wendy S. Delmater

As a trainee safety manager I was studying Federal OSHA and EPA regulations, as well as New York State safety-related laws concerning everything from asbestos & lead removal to the transportation of hazardous materials. But it seemed that New York City had its *own* safety laws, which were all about protecting the adjacent buildings and property. New York *City's* safety laws as well as federal and state safety laws were upheld by a *severely* understaffed position called "Site Safety Manager." That was my goal, then, to become an NYC licensed Site Safety Manager. The question then became, how to go about becoming one?

An NYC site safety manager's license required a 40-hour course and an exam. To sit for the exam, you needed to have eight years of verifiable work in heavy construction on a what they called a "major building," or only four years experience if you had a degree in safety or a related field. At the time, NYC defined a major building as a construction project that was at least eight stories high or had a footprint of at least half a city block. One of the buildings on our multi-building courthouse project was going to be eight stories tall and the project was slated to run three years! It was a good start.

Due to the severe shortage of construction safety managers, my employer sent me to a week-long crash safety management course at the National Safety Council, then in Chicago. I had a marvelous trip where learned a great deal in a class full of others who loved this subject. I missed my gradeschool-aged sons very much but my sister watched them for me.

I learned the history of the safety movement in the United States. Around the turn of the century, several disasters happened at the dawn of our Industrial Revolution. First there was the Great Chicago Fire of 1870: the main problem that caused it to spread so far was not Mrs. O'Leary's cow knocking over a lantern, it was the fact that all of the responding fire departments had different diameter hoses with different couplings. Railroad, mining and steel production in brought a tremendous increase in accidents, and unions formed. Then there was the Triangle Shirtwaist Factory fire, an avoidable tragedy that could have been prevented by unblocked, unlocked fire exits. 145 young women died, and the public was outraged. Insurance, which only used to cover property, started to cover people. Worker's Compensation insurance, which started in Europe, made its way to the USA, state by state.

Confessions of a Female Safety Engineer

The history of safety management was one long bloody march from uncaring employers who felt a few deaths and disfigurements were "the cost of doing business" to an outraged public insisting that such a cost was absolutely unacceptable. I learned, then, the various ways to protect workers. I'll weave them into real world examples, later in this book.

After the week-long safety course was over, on Friday, I had a day to myself to see the city before I flew back home on Saturday afternoon. I got cheap tickets to the Chicago symphony and went out to eat for dinner, using most of my expense account for that day on a nice meal. I was thrilled to see that some members of my safety class that week were dining at the same restaurant, some executives from United Parcel Service. I tried to join them. Outside of the classroom, however, these men dropped their polite veneer. It was my first encounter with rabid misogyny. Who did I think I was, believing a woman could be a safety manager or even want to talk to exalted *them*? They left the room in a huff, so upset that the maître d' came over to try and smooth the situation. In recompense for my "bad experience" he offered me a voucher for free meal, with wine and dessert. Ha! Thanks, nasty UPS execs!

Then it was time for the symphony. But an elderly man was sleep in my cheap seat. He apologized profusely, explaining that since he was semi-retired he liked to sleep during the performances and no one ever bought this inexpensive seat in the back. He was one of the curators of the *Chicago Field Museum*. As a recompense for taking my seat (there were 30 empty seats nearby, no problem for me I assured him) would I like a personalized tour of *The Field Museum* and *The Art Institute of Chicago* tomorrow, including where they set up the exhibitions in the back? Sure!

So Saturday morning I got a free personalized tour of one of the world's most famous natural history museums. I got to see things most visitors never glimpse, like where they did radioactive carbon dating of artifacts, and how they set up the exhibits. Then my personal docent guide took me through the nearby *Art Institute of Chicago*, which has world-famous pieces like the iconic painting "American Gothic." This was followed by a delicious free lunch with that voucher. I flew home feeling more confident that I knew enough to start making a difference as a safety manager. I was awed that they needed someone to do this sort of work so badly that they'd paid for this marvelous trip.

Back at the construction site where I worked, I studied. I started leading safety meetings for the project management. I learned to read blueprints and all about construction scheduling. I was, nominally, part of the management team and went to job progress meetings.

But my problem was getting out of that construction trailer, and into the field. The safety department might want me, badly. But the project manager wouldn't authorize it.

Because I was female.

THE FIRST HURDLE

THERE WERE FOUR OTHER WOMEN WHO WORKED FOR MY EMPLOYER ON THAT site: the estimator, the human resources manager, the secretary/admin and one of my best friends on the construction site, Lori.

Lori was a younger woman who was a structural engineer. Very brilliant, very nice looking in a girl-nextdoor-cheerleader sort of way, very down to earth. We ate lunch together often and she loved to spoil my sons. I asked her into my plan clerk office and shut the door.

"Lori," I said, "would you believe they won't authorize me going out into the field to do safety work?"

"Why?" she asked, incredulous.

"Because I 'might get hurt.' "

"What??? How old are you?"

"I'm thirty-four," I replied.

Her eyes went huge. "I'll bet they wouldn't say that if you were a guy! What can we-" she snapped her fingers. "I know! Let's have this conversation again outside of Sam's office."

"Deal." We left my office and walked down to the hall between the Dave project engineer's and Sam the project manager's offices. Their doors were open and we could see in passing that Sam was at his desk. We stood just out of sight, but not out of earshot. She nodded for me to begin.

"Lori, they won't authorize me going out into the field to do safety work!"

"Why not?"

"Because they say I 'might get hurt.'"

"Are you kidding? And just how old are you?"

"I'm thirty-four," I replied, sounding very annoyed. All rusting of papers from the boss' office had stopped.

"Thirty-four? Well. I'll bet they wouldn't say that if you were a *guy*, " Lori growled.

"I know. It's ridiculous."

Confessions of a Female Safety Engineer

Lori, eyes sparkling, ended the our mini protest by giving me a thumbs up as she looked at the big boss' office. "Oh, I have to meet someone. Catch you later!" We parted ways, going opposite directions.

I was authorized to go out into the field the next day.

Earning My Spurs

THE NEXT MORNING I WAS CALLED INTO THE DAVE THE PROJECT ENGINEER'S office.

"We're letting you out in the field. Spend the time learning. Your background is in residential remodeling, not heavy construction. So if you are not familiar with a process, stop and ask questions. They have a lot to teach you."

I nodded.

Dave continued, "I've spoken to the superintendents and asked them to meet with you. Here's a radio (a walkie talkie). Here's how the radio works. Be careful using it. Anything you say on this *everyone* else will hear. And you are *not* to stop the work out there except for an IDLH: a situation immediately dangerous to life and health. Got it? Good. Go meet with the superintendents. They're waiting."

I thanked Dave, truly grateful. And I immediately trotted down the hall and two connectors over to the superintendent's trailer, part of a complex of connected trailers required for this immense job. All five supers were there, waiting for me.

Dominating the room was Keith at his desk, the former linebacker head superintendent. Left to right around his desk there was a lanky older gentleman, George, who was in charge of building the new Family Court. Next was quiet creole Guy who was in charge of building new Supreme Court. On the right side of Keith's desk were nondescript Harold who was in charge of building the new Office Building, and lastly fireplug-built Gus who was in charge of the eight-story District Court. I knew them from attending job progress meetings as an observer, and from safety meetings I'd led. Gus's glower said he was not happy to be there.

And rather than feeling intimidated, I knew that people who wanted to do this sort to work were rare, and that they therefore needed me. I held my head high. Anyone new, male or female I reasoned, would have to prove themselves to these very competent men. I was here to learn and I would not be afraid. I

Confessions of a Female Safety Engineer

had children to feed, and I was determined that these men were going to be my allies. They were not going to stand in my way.

Keith, the head super, started the impromptu meeting. He was matter of fact about it all. "Sam and Dave asked us to be a part of your training. So if you run into a problem, a real life and limb problem, and you cannot fix it yourself, you use your radio to call the super of whatever building you're in. And this is a union site. If you see a problem on the site, unless it's something that will get someone *immediately killed or injured*, you find out who the shop steward is and tell *him* about it. Especially with the electricians." Otherwise it was a recap of my instructions from Dave, the project engineer. You're mainly going to be out there to learn, ask questions, and observe. We've been instructed to help.

I accepted the instruction humbly but not in a servile manner.

Keith asked if there were any questions or comments. At that point fireplug Gus unfolded his arms and stood erect from the spot he'd been leaning against on the wall. "I just want to say something," he said with controlled anger. "I don't think women belong out in the field." He was voicing a protest, letting us know he was ordered to do something and he was complying, but resentful. Gus continued, "You're taking away some man's job and I don't like it."

Well. That demanded a response. "Gus," I replied with sympathy, "The person who took that man's job was my ex-husband, who abandoned me with three small children. If you're angry, be angry with him. I'd rather be home baking cookies for my kids, but I need to support them. I'm not doing this to make political points in some sort of Gloria Steinem move. I'm a breadwinner. Just like you." At that point, I was the *sole* breadwinner. Child support, when my ex finally started paying it next month, was $33 per child, per week, and not all that steady. Gus the superintendent could not get in the way of me feeding my kids. I needed to win his trust.

Gus nodded, somewhat mollified but still not happy.

Keith and the others all seemed to relax a fraction, whether in relief that Gus' brewing anger had been dealt with or in respect for my answer. Maybe both. I thanked them all, promised to learn and listen, and left to finish my plan clerk duties. I'd walk out onto the site right after lunch.

14

Wendy S. Delmater

Afternoon. This was it. I'd learned the basic theory, the basic regulations. Now I had permission to learn the hands-on part of construction safety management, in the field. I'd read the floor plans for each building and made up a clipboard with places to put notes about each floor. Every morning once I'd decided on this career path I'd put on my construction boots with the expectation of getting more dirt on them than I'd get on my way from the parking lot to the construction trailer. Today, I finally would.

Tales From a New World

PURPOSEFULLY WALKING THROUGH ALL FOUR BUILDINGS AND THE SURROUNDING construction site took all afternoon.

The first and second days were easy. I noted a loose floor hole cover here, a trip hazard there, a broken safety railing, or bad housekeeping. I gave the report to our labor foreman and he took care of the problems in the morning. Simple. There was an electrician on an A-frame ladder right next to an open, five-story elevator shaft whom I stopped to ask him to tie off. His foreman and shop steward complained about me stopping the work, and Guy, our super for that building, backed me up. It began to feel real.

My baptism by literal fire happened on the third day. No one was there to see it but that was a turning point for me, a moment of intense personal courage that no one else saw, where I asked myself, *Can I do this?* I seriously was not sure I was capable of handling the job.

You see, one of the things no one ever told me, that I should have guessed, was that when you inspect for unsafe things sometimes you'll *find* them. And sometimes someone else's mistakes can put you at risk. Looking back on so many jobs now it seems blindingly obvious that if I was checking for bad electrical cords, I might get shocked. If I was inspecting a scaffold, it might have a loose board or railing that could pitch me to my death. If I was checking for toxic chemicals or asbestos, I might breathe them in. But I didn't know. I didn't know.

I was walking up a partially finished stairwell and suddenly a continuous cascade of molten steel slag spray arched gracefully down, in front and behind me. I stood stock still, terrified, all too easily imagining the steel eating through my clothes and my skin and the horrible burns that would result. I was intensely relieved I was wearing a hard hat and safety glasses, but the rest of me was very much at risk. I forced myself to think rather than panic. I did not want to yell and startle whoever was causing the molten threat; it might jostle his hand and move the fiery spray to where I was. I had to get past my fear and decide which way to go and when to move.

Confessions of a Female Safety Engineer

I forced back my horror as I watched the spray of slag fall mere inches from my face and decided there was a pattern to it, an occasional lull in the rain of fire that would give me enough time to walk up where I could be seen. No one else knew that I had to grow a pair to bull through the hopefully momentary lack of dripping molten steel, to walk up that stairwell and keep my job.

A welder looked up, startled, when he saw me. He was reaching for a welding rod; obviously he'd been welding the stair rails together. I was surprised how steady my voice was when I asked him to close off the stairwell below him so no one would get hit by the slag, as that's procedure. He apologized, moved to do so, and I moved on. No one else knew how changed I was inside. I was committed now. I knew the work could be dangerous, and I wanted to do it anyhow.

Another series of big memories from those early days were all the lessons the simple tradesmen taught me. I tried to follow the project engineer and superintendents' admonitions to watch and learn. But I found that I made men nervous while I was studying, by simple act of watching them. They assumed I was looking for mistakes! I learned to draw the men out, to ask them questions, to compliment what I saw that was correct and good, and use humor. And I learned what *not* to do from some of their complaints and stories about "safety guys" they'd known.

I discovered that construction workers hated the typical safety rep for the following reasons: safety inspectors had no idea how things were built (sequencing and trade work), and they had no idea of what materials and labor cost. I was told that the safety inspectors typically showed up, threw their weight around on power trips, and left delays and chaos in their wake.

Never mind my needing to learn about things like welding and steel erection; *that* was the most important lesson I learned in those early days. Make them glad to see you, know what's going on, find out what various solutions cost, and above all when you need to stop them refer to an outside authority like OSHA, with sympathy. I wasn't *my* fault the insurance company and the government made these rules, but I was there to make sure they got home in one piece, with as little disruption from the "idiot inspectors" as possible. I wasn't one of those "idiot inspectors." I'd run a small construction business, and I knew they were in business to make money. So I learned how much things cost, labor and safety supplies, and the interrelated effects of delays to the schedule. I learned that most of the actual work happened in the morning, and after lunch was mostly set-up time for the next day, so I started inspecting in the morning and doing my plan clerk work in the afternoons.

There were so many laws about so many processes, and I had to make them work with what comedians would call a "tough room." Luckily, I loved challenges

I had a lot to figure out before they would take me seriously, and not all of it was about construction. Some of it was how to deal with being female in an almost all-male field. I needed to learn how to talk their language. I read voraciously on the topic, kept my eyes open, and learned that men are by and large more likely to be linear thinkers who want you to stay on topic. I learned that one of the best ways to get a male to be your friend was to seriously ask his advice about something; that meant you respected him.

But not all men were that way. I learned how to deal with jerks like the unsafe excavator subcontractor whose work I had to stop before he killed someone. I called him into my office where I allowed the head of that unsafe company tell me all of his excuses: why I was wrong and he was right. Then I repeated them back to him so he was sure I understood why he thought it was *perfectly acceptable* to put a man in a ten-foot-deep wet sandy excavation with sheer sides, a too-short ladder, and adjacent traffic. (a.k.a., a death trap.) Being a mother was handy in dealing with this man; I used the "broken record" technique I'd learned for dealing with toddlers on him and kept repeating what the law said, over and over. In response, he tried me buy me off of writing him up by offering me a job as "one of the girls in my office." Nope. I simply gave him a memo citing OSHA's trenching law and his company's infraction, and I sent a carbon copy to my head superintendent, shaking my head. I was frankly not insulted as a woman; I felt sorry for the man because he was a loser. He was not a jerk because he was a man. He was just a jerk.

In situations like this, I very much doubted hiding behind a judge's robes and a discrimination lawsuit would help my career or change these men's ideas about women. After all, I was in a topsy-turvy world where it was polite to leave the toilet seat *up*. It *was* a boy's club. But I liked men, and tried to play by heir rules on their playing field instead of insisting they played by my rules.

Confessions of a Female Safety Engineer

Yet I would not be seen as "merely" a woman. I wanted to be seen as a *person*. I was just me, take it or leave it, but no one's doormat. And if I was going to be me, I was not of the opinion that I had to stop being feminine to be strong. The battle of the sexes, in my opinion, would be about who could be more chivalrous (like me opening doors for men who were carrying heavy things). I decided I'd have to insist on respect to get it, and I quickly realized that men were all about getting respect, too. I could work with that.

So when I was sarcastically called "Sweetheart" in front of witnesses by the project foreman, the man in charge of our laborers, I made a snap decision to give it back in kind. Humor, I reminded myself, is a potent weapon. So I called him Sweetcheeks right in front of those same witnesses. Again, I felt his remark was the sort of hazing any "new guy" might get, but tailored to my gender instead of some other obvious feature like red hair or big feet. And I passed with flying colors, earning his respect.

Tall, elderly George the superintendent was another matter. He was a big supporter of my training but he was of a generation where he called me "Darlin'" from pure reflex. Coming from someone like George I felt such endearments were not disrespectful, but the younger men might take it that way. So I asked him to try not to do that in public and warned him with a twinkle in my eye that if he ever slipped up and called me Darlin' in front of the men, I'd call him Peaches. He blushed, laughed and assured me he would do his best.

Poor old George—very sharp man, I learned a lot from him—sincerely tried to call me by a military sort of ma'am, which I was fine with, or by my name. But one day he slipped and forgot, and called me Darlin' in public, in front of the men. So...yeah. I went there. I blandly called him Peaches in front of the guys with a totally straight poker face.

Later on, I found him in the super's trailer, laughing so hard he was actually crying. "You warned me! You warned me!" he wheezed between laughs. I'm sure the story got around.

And he never forgot to simply use my real name, ever again. Neither did anyone else.

Wendy S. Delmater

Here is how I earned Gus's respect. This story is one of my favorites.

Gus' responsibility was the eight-story building, the District Court, the only one tall enough to require a personnel hoist. A hoist is a bare-bones temporary elevator that runs up the exterior of a tall building until the interior elevators are installed. When I inspected that building at the end of that first week there was a crew dismantling the steel hoist, which had been taken apart down to the fourth floor just below me on the 5th. None of the men taking down the hoist were wearing any safety harnesses and lanyards and they were 45 feet in the air (and you have a 50 percent chance of dying from a 6-ft fall). No fall protection was an IDLH situation. And to make matters worse they were not following any of the other basic safety rules: they were wearing sneakers instead of safety shoes, shorts instead of pants that covered their legs, no hard hats, no safety glasses – nothing. When I asked them to get their safety gear they looked at me long enough to let me know they'd heard me, and then studiously ignored me.

Call it divine inspiration, but this is what I did. I walked around a corner far enough they could not hear me, pulled my radio out of its holster, and called my arch nemesis, the hostile superintendent Gus. "Gus? I have a situation I need your help with, on the 5th floor of the District Court building, on the west side by the hoist. Can you meet me here? Five minutes? Great. " Then I looked at my watch for the time, and walked back out to watch the hoist guys misbehave.

Exactly four minutes later, I drawled cheerfully, "Hey guys, perhaps I should have mentioned that the building superintendent Gus is on his way here." I looked down at my watch. "In fact, he should be here any second." Now, what they were doing was wrong and they knew it. And Gus approved whether their company got paid. He could throw workers off the site. They might not respect me, but they sure as hell respected and feared Gus. So they all gave me poisonous looks, but they climbed down the steel frame on the double and went to their nearby cars to find and start donning the proper safety equipment.

Right about then, Gus showed up. He looked down at the partially dismantled hoist, then back to where I was still casually leaning on the safety railing.

The hoist guys looked up, saw me with Gus, and put their safety gear on faster.

"Where is everybody?" Gus asked.

Confessions of a Female Safety Engineer

Me, offhandedly, "I believe they climbed down to go put on their safety gear." Which, as Gus could see, was the truth. He paused and watched them for a minute, then nodded curtly. "Good," he said.

Looking up from the ground, the hoist disassembly crew was convinced that Gus would back me up and that I had his authority. But more importantly, Gus was convinced I'd persuaded that very rough crew of men to accept my authority without him showing up.

Timing, as they say, is everything.

One more tale from the early days. There was a man using a cutting torch in a open, partly-finished steel-framed building, above another set of oxygen and acetylene bottles on a cart, chained to a pillar below him. The slag had been falling on the volatile compressed oxygen and acetylene tanks. The man was ordered by me to move from his position several floors above the oxy/acetylene set up below his work, or go down there and move the cart. So he stopped, and assured me that he would not work above the tanks. And I moved on.

As soon as I was out of the area he must have resumed his risky behavior. And, sure enough, a piece of hot slag fell on a weak spot on the neck of the acetylene tank, burned through, and set it on fire. It became a tall blowtorch that burned through three floors of erected steel. We had to evacuate the whole site in case the attached oxygen tank blew a huge crater into the ground. We waited at a safe distance until the acetylene burned out, and then a while longer until the fire cooled.

I knew who'd done it and was involved in writing up my first incident report. I had done my job, and it was not my fault I was disregarded. The company's safety management was immensely pleased with my work. To cap the week, the night security guard had a heart attack and I, with my recent CPR training, waited with him until the ambulance came. In the thank you note I got the next week, the man credited me with saving his life by keeping him calm. I still have his note, and I treasure it.

When things were quiet, I organized our chemical safety Material Safety Data Sheets and made a spreadsheet so we could find them easily. I hounded the subcontractors until they all turned in a safety training sessions on topics I sent out, based on current and coming hazards on the schedule, and then inspected to see if they had really learned anything. I made sure everyone had a safety orientation with documentation.

Wendy S. Delmater

It was well that I had gotten into a good routine and mindset before our site was chosen for a rather dubious honor. OSHA wanted to do a long-term study, and chose our site to do it. With video cameras. For months.

Smile! You're on Camera

ONE FINE DAY, WE HAD A FEDERAL OCCUPATIONAL SAFETY AND HEALTH inspection. Now an OSHA inspection is enough to make a strong man quail, as their fines are immense, they disrupt your routine (all the minor subs go home since it's not worth the risk), and they can tie you up in expensive litigation. The standard way to deal with an OSHA inspection is to tell them you'll call your safety director, make the team of two inspectors wait for the safety director to come, and while the inspectors are waiting get your crew to frantically make sure everything on your site is as safe as you can make it. I was sent out to check on things and missed the "opening conference" where OSHA tells you why they are there. Was it a random audit, a visit due to a complaint, or something computer generated based on our company's previous history with OSHA?

None of the above. They wanted to do a study on how much of safety on a big construction site was up to the general contractor, and how much was up to the subcontractors. And we caught their eye because one of the inspectors drove by our site every day on his way home. We'd won the scrutiny lottery simply by being in the right place at the right time. Joy.

At first, the corporate safety manager walked with them. But after a few days it was obvious the OSHA inspectors would be there a long time. And the safety manager was running more than one job so he could not accompany them every day. Therefore, I—the *assistant* safety manager, the trainee—was asked to walk the site with the OSHA inspectors. My instructions were, "If they take a photo of something, you take a photo of it, too. If they made a video of something, you make a video of the same thing, preferably from as close to the same angle at the same time as possible." The project engineer gave me a new video camera to go with my company digital camera. I practiced with the video camera until I was comfortable with it.

It was a pretty tense situation. Once a mistake was on film a fine was virtually guaranteed, and many of our subs were caught red handed doing

25

things like leaving down guardrails or not wearing hard hats; delivery people were particularly fined for not wearing hard hats when they got out of their vehicles until I called all of our vendors and raised the roof. The OSHA inspectors did not catch my men in any bad situations but I was nervous. We were not perfect, and the longer they were there the higher the chance they'd catch us out.

Imagine driving cross-country with two cop cars on your bumper, waiting to ticket you if you made the least little mistake. That's what it felt like. This went on for three days a week. For two-and-a-half *months*.

So it was time for some people skills.

Rather than have them look around for things to write up, I pumped the OSHA inspectors for all of the great stories they could tell me, and they had seen quite a few things that were instructive. They'd investigated overturned cranes, and shared ways to keep a crane from tipping. They'd seen electric cutting tool disks shatter, and people lose their eyesight; here was how to avoid that. We talked about typical recordkeeping things that got construction companies OSHA fines, and how to avoid fines.

Asking them to share their safety stories was not exactly a ploy, as I was really interested in what they taught me, but in a way it was a tactic. Everyone thinks you're really nice and really smart if you're a good listener! Then they like you, so they are less likely to write you up. When they ran out of construction anecdotes, I steered our conversation to talk about our families, and then about our hobbies. I discovered that we were all hobby fishermen and we talked merrily about favorite fishing spots and bait and "the one that got away."

I think the hairiest time during that inspection was when the compressed gas vendor made a disastrous delivery. The site administrative assistant, of all people, signed for a delivery of full-sized oxygen and acetylene cylinders. These cylinders are supposed to be kept separate by gas type, and separated by either a firewall or a distance of 20 feet. The cylinders are supposed to be stored upright, and secured.

Instead, the vendor had left the tanks in a mixed group together, unsecured and drunkenly tilted in the sand. *Leaning up against the OSHA inspectors' car.* The two OSHA inspectors and I came back to the office from the field and we just stared at the cylinders. "Oh dear," I mumbled, embarrassed, and called our foreman to fix it while the inspectors watched. Then the inspectors, without filming the error, watched me go in and explain to the secretary that she was not authorized to sign for compressed gasses. She had to call a foreman, a superintendent, or project management to sign for them and make sure the tanks were stored safely. Finally, I called that compressed gas vendor and told them that if they ever made such a sloppy delivery again, we'd take our business elsewhere. The OSHA inspectors and I all got a good laugh and they were impressed. "*That's* how you handle such a situation," they complimented me. No write up. No fine. I was their protégé. They were proud of me!

I will never forget how the project engineer and project manager both nearly fainted when I told them where and how the OSHA inspectors and I found those compressed gas cylinders. And their relief plus the growing respect in their eyes when I explained how I'd built relationships with those inspectors so the company would *not* be written up.

I had not been invited to the opening conference, but the company sure wanted me to come to the OSHA closing conference. We ran a very safe site but if these inspectors had wanted to find something they always could. OSHA would not find something to write up because we ran a safe site and I'd requested these men help with my training. They were now my mentors and *friends.*

And that was another big early lesson I learned. The books I read said women are all about relationships and men were all about jockeying for dominance. I discovered, that, male or female, it's *all* about relationships.

My company came out of the OSHA study with no fines and one *de minimis* violation, a mere slap on the wrist. (Many of our subs who would not listen to me were not so lucky.) And at the end of the inspection period, these same OSHA inspectors sponsored me into the prestigious American Society of Safety Engineers (ASSE).

CAN YOU TOP THIS DARWIN AWARD?

HANGING OUT WITH OTHER SAFETY ENGINEERS AT THE NATIONAL SAFETY Council, or at ASSE meetings, was an amazing experience. They told such *great* stories. And although there were a lot of laughs at the Darwin Award tryouts we'd seen or heard of at our businesses or on our sites, we had serious reasons for sharing crazy safety situations or violations. These were cautionary tales, things you could use as examples in safety training, to help run safe jobs.

So when one safety manager talked about how they'd broken something, you might laugh but you took mental notes.

For example, there was that site in NYC where they had drilled into solid rock to place charges and excavate out a foundation. The safety manager had very carefully had the general contractor cover the blast area with anchored, strong netting – to catch any rocks that might go airborne. And it worked, the first time. But the second blast area was nextdoor to the first one, and rather than loose the anchors on all four corners they just loosed the far ones, and flipped the netting over.

Of course this meant that any rocks embedded in the netting from the first blast went flying with the next blast. They broke about a hundred windows on an adjacent skyscraper. Oops. Lesson learned? Pretty obvious.

Some of the stories were just funny, like the safety manager working in a hospital who had to ask his crews to stop buying food from a particular Chinese restaurant, because that takeout place used red bags, and they were renovating a hospital. "Red-bag" waste in a hospital was the designation for getting rid of potentially infectious things like used needles and bloody bandages, and the poor hospital as paying exorbitant fees to get rid of anything in a red bag, including their Chinese food leftovers.

Lesson learned? Don't bring anything in a red plastic bag to a hospital or you will cause your customer unnecessary expense.

There was the tale of the two men standing side-by-side, one drilling into metal with only prescription glasses on and the other with no glasses of any

Confessions of a Female Safety Engineer

kind. Metal shavings were bouncing off of both of their faces and could easily bounce up under the man's reading glasses. "I'm wearing glasses," said the first. "I'm just watching," said the second man. Lesson learned: safety glasses had side shields and men might not think they were necessary, but eye protection was essential. Usually, story one was followed up during eye protection training with a story about a guy who was not so lucky and lost an eye.

You could use a story like that in a safety talk with the men to illustrate the need for safety glasses. Human nature being what it is, men will see someone else being a fool before they'll see themselves being a fool.

Tales about of people bungee jumping off cranes, and dying, leading to suppressed news stories so there would be no copycats. Not funny, but here's how you avoid people bungee jumping off of *your* crane on *your* site.

There were tales about how to deal with inspecting agencies, like the time the EPA would not let the New York State Power Authority at Niagara Falls kill the zebra mussels that were clogging their tunnels, so they did an end-run around the EPA and make the water potable before it went through the pipes, drinkable germ-free water which killed the mussels as a side effect.

Lesson learned, use an agency's own rules against it.

We'd circulate pictures, too, of things like a cutting disk shattered and embedded in a face shield, and use the illustration to train our men on how to use that tool safely. (Fact: If the guard won't fit it's probably the wrong-sized abrasive wheel which will cause the abrasive wheel to vibrate and shatter.) Pictures of crane ball-and-hooks that had fractured, dropping their loads. (Lesson learned: stay out from under crane loads!) We'd tell of fires we'd read the investigative reports on, where lives were lost due to blocked and/or locked fire exits. (This happened recently, again, in Oakland CA at that rave in an artist's studio. You think they'd learn.)

A favorite of mine was a good story about what can get caught in construction debris netting. On the underside of the Mianus River Bridge in Connecticut, part of I-95, there was debris netting installed to catch any falling construction materials before they hit the busy waterway underneath. One weekend, the site was closed. The police received a distraught call from some young man's mother that he was going to kill himself, and they were on the lookout for the fellow's car. A vehicle matching that description and plate number was abandoned on the Mianus River Bridge, in the closed construction area. When they peered over the edge, there was the young man, caught in the debris netting. "I can't even kill myself right!" the fellow moaned. In one of the few times you could actually see a safety program save a life, they got him out and got him help.

That story is not only funny, it's also particularly useful for safety managers that are discouraged. Usually we can only track how many lives are saved and injuries are avoided via statistics. And when no one is getting hurt because we are doing our job correctly, most employers start to resent the expense of a safety program. Once in a while it's nice to know for a certainty that doing the right thing saves lives.

One OSHA investigator had been at the crater of what was once a company that bottled oxygen, another at the site of a former fireworks factory. Both incidents involved tremendous loss of life had been set off by sparks from static electricity, probably from shoes. Great stories for safety training about working with compressed oxygen or in a spark-free environment.

Perhaps the most impressive story we talked about was the 32-page investigative report on how the space shuttle Challenger accident happened. It was titled, "The Silent Safety Program, " and it detailed how a root-cause analysis of what went wrong found out it was related to layoffs at NASA. The men in the field building the shuttle knew about the problem with the O-ring that eventually was the obvious, proximate cause of the explosion. They reported it up the chain of command. But the chain was broken in several places, and their reports about their concerns with the O-ring landed on the desks of people who'd been laid off. The reports languished on several desks, but went no further.

Lesson learned, always know your chain of command, and follow up.

Or things could go boom.

All Good Things Come To An End

My OSHA experience was what you'd call a résumé builder. I was increasingly sure I'd found my calling. My sons were proud of me, and I was able to pick them up right after school, or shortly after they were bused to an afterschool program. If I had to work very late I could bring them to the jobsite and they'd do homework or color in the conference room. Their art soon decorated project management's offices.

The rest of the courthouse project was a blur of learning, friendship, and mostly good experiences. And since I loved to write I started working with the General Contractor's newsletter editor, doing articles highlighting safety. I started turning my notes from safety training sessions, which I was too inexperienced to realize were highly innovative, into articles for the regional ASSE group, which got forwarded to their national construction division newsletter. This lead to my being asked to do a two-year stint as the ASSE's Construction Division Newsletter editor.

That was fun. The outgoing editor complained that getting articles was like pulling teeth, and handed me a list of safety engineers who might, just might write me an article if pushed. Really? Since it would cut my work experience requirement for sitting for the NYC Site Safety manager's license exam in half I was considering getting a degree in safety. I had a list of ASSE-affiliated colleges and universities. Those schools were chock full of "publish or perish" professors, grad students, and students – all writing papers anyhow. I contacted them. Pretty soon I was turning away articles and was able to theme my issues.

I made a lot of friends in the local ASSE chapter, too, people who had been in the safety field for years and worked at places as diverse as an international cosmetics factory, a large interstate bakery, Brookhaven National Laboratory, and Cold Spring Harbor Labs. Some of them enjoyed mentoring me. I was usually the only woman at the meetings but I didn't care. These were people who loved the same things I loved. It was like coming home.

Confessions of a Female Safety Engineer

They helped me with my résumé. But as the big construction project I was on started to wind down, I could not find another job in my field on Long Island, in New York City, or even in nearby states. They all required a degree. And I was not able to find a *local* college that taught safety: all of them seemed to be in Illinois, California, or Florida.

Right before the project ended, my construction friends like Lori helped my sons and I to move out of our foreclosed home into a tiny apartment which had insects and turned out to be in an unsafe neighborhood. But it was all I could afford. Our world got much smaller.

When the project ended, I spent an uncomfortable month on unemployment looking for a job related to safety management until I realized that I'd have to go back to temping. I still wrote and edited for ASSE but it seemed futile. There'd be no more safety work without a degree and I could not find a college I could *get to* that offered my major. It was a time of defeat. I felt like my dream was dying.

Reluctantly, I went back to being an office temporary. The first agency I registered with immediately placed me at a large construction site in nearby Nassau County, where a general contractor was building a new research and manufacturing facility. I was the site secretary/admin. It was very, very frustrating. Two of the top men on staff were serial philanderers and part of my job was to keep their girlfriends and wives apart! Luckily the construction company's NY district safety director came to inspect the site, and he recognized my name from my ASSE writing and editing work. What was I doing working as an admin? Well, I couldn't find a nearby college that taught safety!

So he sent me to where he got his degree. He told me of a local college that taught safety management, Mercy College. I looked them up. While not ASSE-affiliated, Mercy College was within driving distance. They had a lot of evening courses and two majors that would suit me. They had campuses in Dobbs Ferry NY, the Bronx, in White Plains, and offered a lot of online courses. I applied immediately.

Meanwhile, this site had an OSHA inspection, too. Despite me finding out that the inspection had been triggered by the bad safety record of the company they were building it *for*, nothing I told site management could dissuade them from the believing that I had somehow called OSHA down on them.

Wendy S. Delmater

Office temps' lives are precarious. I was wrongly accused and let go.

But I got my acceptance to Mercy College. From then on, while I finished my degree I temped, temped, and took more jobs as a temp. I gave preference to temp jobs where I could learn something safety-related, like a stint at a fire protection sprinkler company, a titanium foundry, or a manufacturing plant. I refused several full-time positions that were not in my field, and not just because they paid a pittance. Pay was not the only issue; I would not lie about my goals to get hired and then leave them when I finished school.

My sons, aged 10-through thirteen, who'd played in a ball pit at the local McDonalds when I first started studying for the Alliance of American Insurer course, now saw me doing my college homework alongside their junior high school work. They told me I was a weird mom, but a cool one. I was a writer and studying safety in college, so even though I was just an office temp they were proud of me.

I took my boys on a trip to an amusement park and all I wanted to do was look at the safety of the rides. I was told the safest ride in the park was the bungee jumping, so of course I had to check it out. There were inflated pillows like stunt men used and workers safety-spotting you at the base. Workers inside weighed you, put a proper safety harness for your weight on you, had three people sign off that you were outfitted correctly, and then a spotter at the top made sure you were facing toward the central tower so that your "startle" reaction would not cause you to arch your back and then crack your head on the steel platform. Walking backwards off that platform was terrifying, but when that elastic pulled me back up it was the most fun I'd ever had.

My kids introduced me to their friends as, "This is my mom. She bungee jumps" for *years* after that.

WHAT IS THIS 'SLEEP'
OF WHICH YOU SPEAK?

MERCY COLLEGE WAS GREAT. IT WAS AND IS GEARED TOWARD THOSE WHO GO back to school to get a degree in midlife. They accepted 33 of the 34 credits I had earned in my year at Michigan State, and the student loans went through without a hitch. I could take about half of my courses online, but the rest required my physical attendance.

The main campus, in Dobs Ferry, shared a border with Washington Irving's estate and historic site, which I took my sons to see. It was nestled along the lower Hudson River just above the populous areas of the New York Metro area. There was a campus in White Plains, NY, a city a little north of that. There was a campus near the Bronx Zoo that had classes on Saturdays, and I brought my gleeful sons with me on those trips; they were old enough to visit the zoo on their own, now. The main campus for my major, however, was in Yorktown Heights, NY – across the Hudson River from Bear Mountain. That was way the heck in upstate New York, and when we'd get rain near the seacoast, they'd get snow. But I was already halfway to my evening classes up north if I left from most of my temp jobs. It was good that my eldest turned 14 when I started back to school. I could not legally have gone to evening classes before then without a babysitter.

My sons, by the way, were enthusiastic supporters of my getting a degree. They were proud of me as a safety writer and editor, too, and knew my degree would mean financial security for us all. I was also trying to model goal-oriented behavior to them. I had a poster in our house that said, "You can let things happen or you can make things happen." I was trying to model a life that made things happen, and they got the message. They were good kids, and started to make things happen in their own lives. My eldest, Dan, overcame his learning disability and was mainstreamed in school. My middle son, Chris, became interested in Photoshop and graphic design. My youngest, Jon, aimed himself at a business major with dreams of becoming an entrepreneur.

It was still quite a schedule for me, even with supportive neighbors checking in on the kids and life hacks like buying Chinese food on special at lunch and storing it with cold blocks so I could bring it home to heat up for dinner. But I could rarely afford such treats. The stress of poverty was a further drag on my energy. In my second year at Mercy College more than half of the courses were way upstate in Yorktown Heights and the commute plus the temp work plus being a parent to teens became too much.

I had to take a year off of school because I nearly put myself in the hospital from exhaustion. I had three jobs: full-time temping, college, and being a single parent. What was worse, my eldest son had a physical handicap with his severe learning disability, Attention Deficit Disorder without hyperactivity, also known as ADD. While the school had "mainstreamed him" for the physical handicap, they would not admit he had a learning disability. And because of his ADD what would be 15 minutes worth of homework help for a normal child had always run into 2-hours at home. It got only slightly better when he hit puberty.

Things resolved themselves when my eldest son decided to live with his father so he could go to school in Florida, where they would work with his learning disability. My sister let us rent part of her new home in a much safer neighborhood, too.

When I went back to Mercy College a year later, things were out of synch for my major and I had to take some environmental classes at a different college to finish courses Mercy College no longer offered. The loan for that would not fold into my main student loan. I was so poor I had to defer payments, often, just to take care of my sons.

When I was just a few credits away from graduating, I found a safety management job with a general contractor. No more temping! And I hoped that the safety manager position with this contractor would fulfill that last year of experience on a major building that I needed. Then I could sit for the licensed Site Safety Manager exam once I got that degree.

The only problem was that this safety management job was in New Jersey, on the other side of New York City from where I lived. Oh, and it was on the graveyard shift.

BACK IN THE SADDLE

I TOOK THE CONSTRUCTION SAFETY MANAGER POSITION IN NEW JERSEY TO GET the last year of experience needed to work on a major building. "Major building" if you recall, also included the footprint of a project. This site qualified as it stretched along ten miles of railroad track.

It was a pretty nasty job: dangerous precast concrete construction of the new Secaucus Junction Station, mostly lifted into place with huge cranes but also poured in place, all over live tracks on Amtrak's Northeast Corridor. God forbid anything hit those electrified tracks or that we ran late and held up the trains! There were flagmen everywhere and all the lifts were on a very tight schedule. Since it was cold out, I was in charge of making sure the temporary heat used to cure the concrete was done safely, too.

The work ran from 11 PM to 7 AM, in full view of a prison, in the dead of winter with no heat in my company vehicle. Plus, the safety guy on the day shift was...shifty. It meant I had to make 140-mile-round-trip daily commutes so unbelievable that GEICO audited me to make sure I was not living in NJ where they did not offer car insurance. I even had to make this round-trip commute on days when we could not work due to rain not being a good mix with electrified tracks. I'd get paid for the day, but only if I drove in and waited around until Amtrak released us.

I got to the point where I would order dinner at a 24-hour diner just to eat something other than eggs when I got off work at 7 AM.

But I wanted that NYC Site Safety Manager's license. It was the ticket to financial security for us.

Some interesting things happened on that site. I worked with the biggest crane I had ever seen in my life, a 500-ton Manitowoc lattice boom crawler crane that ran on treads like a tank; its reeving (the way the steel cables are arrayed and wound to handle loads) was absolutely fascinating to me. I'd done crane safety before but not like this. It was a beast, and its operator was an artist at setting those huge precast concrete pieces above the tracks. The procedure for deicing his crane's treads alone was amazing.

39

Confessions of a Female Safety Engineer

I had to deal with workers who needed a place to de-ice as well, and the contractor provided a heated shed for them to thaw out as needed. The winter was brutal. But by now I realized I really loved working out of doors, in almost any weather. Working with Amtrak was a revelation, too; I found that I *loved* working in a rail environment. I soaked up what they taught me about things like railway flagging, signaling, and railway crash barricades like a sponge. I learned that the rails are not under OSHA, they are under the Federal Railway Authority or FRA. Very similar rules, except for quirks like the FRA allowing open fires. I guess if they're out in the middle of nowhere the railroad workers needed to keep warm.

Somehow, I survived my four months on the graveyard shift. I was transferred to a nearby project on the day shift. This job was another one with a large footprint, although this was mostly bridge and highway work. The $87-million-dollar undertaking connected an exit off the NJ Turnpike, just south of Newark International Airport, to Route US-1 and to access a new mall they were building on an old landfill. I had to drive over 11 miles just to inspect all the not-yet-connected parts of the project.

I still only had three-plus years' experience in construction safety so there was still a lot to learn. I was trained on how to train the fit-testing of respirator masks, how to calibrate air quality sensors, supervised my first confined space entry, and got experience in other vital things.

The work was unexpectedly challenging. They'd recently found buried chlorine tanks during an excavation and had quite a dangerous time there. While my predecessor had handled *that* well he was an environmental guy who had let site safety run amok during his tenure. He'd pretty much just sat in his the construction trailer doing volunteer phone work for a charity. I quickly got the message that they did not want an actual safety manager, they wanted a yes-man, a rubber stamp who would look the other way while they repeatedly cut corners on safety and put workers at risk. To me, that was unacceptable.

I arrived when the site was doing the largest dynamic soil compaction project in the history of the world. This process involved heavy weights repeatedly dropped by cranes, then lifted and dropped again. There were nearly 100 cranes dropping weights all around the site, compacting the landfill. And the soil was rocky. Softball and brick-sized rocks were flying *everywhere*, but site management did not seem to think that was a problem, even after huge rocks went through the windshields of employees' cars. Project management finally followed some of my advice when a rock went through their office window during a meeting. My solution was get them to order the cranes positioned so they stood with their backs to the construction trailers and so that any rocks headed our way would be blocked by the machines. The operators were already protected, and the rocks would then spray away from us. But even getting them to do *that* simple thing took argument.

Such flagrant flouting of safety rules was a top-down phenomenon, driven by the immense profits to be made on this 'design-build' job. Their contract specified that certain things had to be built, but not *how*. So the contractor saved money in legitimate ways, through design and materials innovations. For example, the contract specified that they had to build overpasses but not the method of construction. The usual way of building slim walls for ramp embankment which would have that amount of heavy traffic was to build reinforced concrete retaining walls. Instead, they got approval to use what was at that point in time new technology: Mechanically Stabilized Earth (MSE) Walls.

These MSE wall used the weight of the soil on interlocking concrete sections that went sideways, deep into the earth mound, to hold the wall in place. From the outside the wall looked like a series of hexagons with wide bases, but those base sections went twelve to fifteen feet inside the hill. It was structurally equal to a reinforced concrete wall for less than a third of the cost.

Unfortunately, the contractor also saved money by cutting corners on worker safety. Employers like this were why OSHA regulations were written and necessary. The tiny, brilliant but amoral female project manager was corporate's darling, since she made them *so much money*. She was used to doing everything her way. We became enemies, barely tolerating each other.

In the battles that ensued, and there were many, I discovered that this company's absolutely fantastic Corporate Safety Director—someone at the *Director* level, just below a VP—only had political power within the company equivalent to one of the project superintendents. So when the safety director tried to advocate for me he was constantly overruled. Resistance to doing the right thing on that site was so strong I had a 75-lb tank of acetylene *thrown* at me by one of their younger supers, and when the safety director complained about it he was told at first that I probably deserved it. Money talked.

And people learned that I *did* know how to swear when someone's life was at stake.

I'm not saying the safety on that site was nonexistent, for most of the supers and foremen and subs wanted to do the right thing, but if it cost money in labor or materials then support was grudging. I learned that my camera was my friend because nothing I said was necessary but cost money was believed without photographic evidence. Subcontractors even offered me bribes to look the other way on potentially lethal safety issues. I took photos of any bad conditions and forced the General Contractor (GC), my employer, to deal with things.

Probably the thing that bothered me the most about this site was the tacit direction that *legitimate claims* of people hurt by their negligence were not to be covered. Now you have to understand that a safety manager's performance, like a golfer's, is judged based on how low their number are. The way it's supposed to work is that you run a safe site, and no one gets hurt, so things like the number of injuries, how many lost work days, and any property damage claims, stay low – and therefore insurance costs stay low. But there is another, darker way to keep injuries low. Don't spend money on safety and then when people get hurt just deny their claims. That was what I was up against, here.

I did make somewhat of a difference, but it usually involved things that cost them no money. A good example was that I did an inventory of all the chemicals on site, got their safety information (which you're supposed to have on file anyhow with documents called Material Safety Data Sheets, or MSDS) and made sure incompatible things were not stored next to each other. I saved a suicidal man, and anyone near him: his wife had just left him and he was cleaning parts in raw gasoline while smoking near a gasoline refueling tank. Things like that.

One humorous incident involved me driving an insurance inspector around the site for his monthly safety inspection. These were scheduled inspections, so the company had things ready for him and would put their best foot forward to get lower rates. This particular time, we got out of the company vehicle where a road stopped and climbed up a ladder to see where it would eventually connect, on the other side of what would become a traffic overpass. This part of the project had crane height restrictions due to it being below the final approach to a runway at Newark International Airport. The planes already had their landing gear down. They flew so low that if you pumped your fist they could see you and they'd honk their horns.

Someone had wanted that ambiance. We came up over the top of a ladder to an amazing scene. An unauthorized Indie film crew had set up on our site in this remote area, and were shooting a movie. The camera was atop an unstable pile of stacked things, not a scaffold, for height. There was a commissary table to the other side serving catered food. And in the middle, an older convertible automobile held an actor and an actress driving toward us. There were pyrotechnics—intentionally detonated explosions—under the car's hood, and the actors were being filmed as the car came to a carefully orchestrated stop.

The insurance inspector was simultaneously horrified and amused. He took a lot of pictures.

Needless to say, they'd not gotten permission to shoot their movie from us, nor would they get it. I shut them down, hard. But I always wondered if they ever finished their movie.

I was a bad safety manager, though. I took people to the emergency room and admitted legitimate claims, which got me in trouble. My "numbers" were bad. Then shifty daytime safety guy at the previous Amtrak site sent his men to me after they were injured and lied about them getting hurt on MY site. He left the company with "zero accidents" on his resume and a glowing recommendation. I was let go when the company moved all their personnel to a job in Queens, ostensibly because that required the site safety manager license I did not have yet. The real reason is that I wouldn't play by their rules.

I still needed a few more months of experience to qualify to sit for the NYC Site Safety Manager's exam, especially since they changed the height requirement on a "major building" to 15 floors. But I vowed I'd never work for a GC or construction manager again. Instead, I looked for safety *consulting* job where due to the shortage I could walk away, or threaten to walk away from unethical contractors and keep my honor. Consulting paid a little less money, but I thought the fact that I could walk away from conflicts of interest made it more principled.

Confessions of a Female Safety Engineer

I found such a position. And after commuting from Long Island, NY to NJ for almost a year, working for a safety consulting company based in New England that at least had a lot of work in the NY metro area did not seem like that much of a stretch.

THE CONSULTING YEARS

I ENJOYED WORKING AS A SAFETY CONSULTANT. MOST OF MY WORK FOR THE New England firm was in industrial safety, with me acting as an insurance inspector or doing things that companies needed an outside expert on, such as specialty safety inspections or specialty mandatory safety training. I learned a great deal during my tenure there. Consulting at colleges, industrial maintenance facilities, and labs broadened my experience. I handled everything from fire safety, to asbestos encapsulation, to hazardous materials, to lab safety, to protecting a remote campus construction site from kids cutting through to go cow tipping.

It was 1998. One of my clients was a building cleaning and maintenance company that had bought a rival and was integrating a 60-person maintenance crew at the World Trade Center, about a year after they'd had that first terrorist explosion in their parking garage.

And it was on this job I ran into the attitude that safety people were not all that important for the very first time.

You see, in 1993 there had been a terrorist attack on the parking garage level, a van with a bomb that had done damage but not as much damage as the terrorists had hoped. After that, you had to have a special pass to get into the twin towers, or show ID and have someone come out to get you. My client would make me wait over an hour to come out and escort me in.

I called the head of the New England safety consulting firm and made sure he was cool with me charging this customer from when they were notified I was there. Then, when they finally bothered to come and bring me in, I informed them that I had been on the clock for the last 50 minutes, since they knew I was waiting. I must say, they were pretty quick to come out and get me after that, when they realized my time was valuable.

It took me two weeks just to inspect the mechanical spaces of both towers. There was the exterior elevator for window washing, way above the observation deck, so high up you could see the curvature of the earth. I saw overhead cranes left in the basement that had been used to bring in materials when the Towers were built. I was shown the entrance to an FBI firing range in a sub basement, and there were five levels of basements. There was a subterranean mall between the two towers that was not our responsibility . I remember not being allowed into two other areas: the Windows on the World restaurant and what rumor said was perhaps a gold vault.

It was one of the few buildings in the world that had two huge physical plants for heating and cooling, one that ran the buildings while the old one was repaired after the '93 attack, and the repaired one. I suggested little improvements like not having a Class A (water only) fire extinguisher near the high voltage equipment (water and electricity are a bad mix) and mandatory hearing protection in the area where that high voltage loudly hummed.

One wild thing I oversaw was the cleaning of the four-foot interior dimension pipes that ran Hudson River water through their repaired basement plant, to cool the buildings. These immense pipes would get mineral scale in them and every so often a person with NO tendency toward claustrophobia wearing a supplied-air respirator would venture in there to de-scale the pipes. He wore an emergency extraction device and had continuous radio contact, and it was run safely by the book, but you could not have paid me enough to do that work.

I also did safety audits of four tradesmen shop areas and did Job Hazard Analyses for repetitive tasks, outlining how to do certain potentially dangerous things safely. The client had crews of HVAC guys, plumbers, electricians and carpenters to maintain the hidden infrastructure of the two towers: the equivalent of a small city. I spent a lot of time getting the previous company's safety records in order, too. These records were a mess. I was sorting through things like accident reports that merely stated "Hurt head" which could be anything from a paper cut to a decapitation.

Perhaps the most poignant thing that happened during my audits of the World Trade Center was that someone on an unaffiliated construction project inside one of the towers died. One of "my" men was close friends with the man who was crushed, and his friend had died in his arms. It was the first time I had to comfort anyone who'd lost a comrade at what I considered to be a sloppily-run construction site. It hardened my conviction that none of "my" men would suffer or die like that.

Years later, I recalled the eerie ceramic eye designs in the E subway station below the towers, and how I thought they'd make creepy ruins. But I heard that "my" men got out on 9/11. The whole crew got out.

My previous work training them in emergency evacuation nothing to do with it, though. They were union workers, and I hear they'd been on strike.

⚠

There were other, resume-enhancing postings while I worked for the New England safety consulting firm. I worked with Ciba-Geigy and at IBM, and consulted at a wastewater treatment plant.

As a bonus, my new employer worked with me on the first part of a two-part work/study college course. This was important, because by now this was all that was standing between me and my degree.

But the New England consulting company was undercapitalized. Upon hiring I was promised 20 hours a week at first, and that the position would eventually become a full-time one. That never happened. In fact, they struggled to give me the 20 hours, and started stinting on expenses even though the jobs got further and further away, deeper into New England. One particularly egregious example was that I was told I could not charge a hotel room, but would have to drive home and back again to a client that was 163 miles each way. (I slept in my car, instead, and almost froze.) Then I was told I would only get 20 hours *if I started to bring in business*. The owner and I parted ways, never saying a bad word to the outside world about each other, but not happy with the situation.

This was right after my mother and sons attended my graduation ceremony; sadly, my father had died several years ago, when I was back to temping. My sons and mother were so proud of me, and took me out to dinner, but I did not actually have my diploma yet.

Now that I had been through my graduation ceremony, all I needed were three more credits in the second part of the work/study course to get my sheepskin. And then, to work, I needed that 40-hour NYC Site Safety Manager (SSM) course and exam. One of the places that offered that course said that if I passed the SSM test and worked for them for three years after I got my license, they'd pay the $2,000 for the course and hire me. Sign me up!

Confessions of a Female Safety Engineer

The exam was supposed to be brutal, with odd things to memorize like terminology that dated back to the previous century. Example: cars were called "power buggies" in NYC safety law. I studied, hard. And during the 40-hour course I had my first encounters with the man who would eventually become my supervisor, a bane of my existence who was another one of those guys who felt that "women did not belong out in the field." During the site safety course this fellow, we'll call him John, did things to try and dissuade me.

But remember when I said my father had been a bitter, vindictive man who took out his frustrations on his family? I'd been worked over by better experts than John.

Early on in the 40-hour class, John tried to gross me out by putting up a slide of someone who'd splattered on the pavement after a fall off a high rise. What he did not know was that the only blood that bothers me is *mine*, or blood from an injury I could have prevented. This was neither.

"So," John leered at me with glee, fully expecting me to freak out, throw up, or pass out, "What does this photo tell you?" I did not even have to pretend to be unruffled. This poor former person was beyond saving, and what had happened to him or her was not my fault.

I studied the slide on the screen dispassionately for a second, and then looked at him calmly and replied in front of the shocked class, "This photo tells me that guts are pink."

He was genuinely surprised at my nonchalance. "Yeah," he admitted. "Yeah, I guess they are. "

During his parts of the 40-hour course he kept trying to trip me up. Instead I kept proving I knew more than anyone else in the room, and they were all men. It got to the point where I had to wait and see if anyone else knew the answers, so I would not always be the one responding.

For example, in the module on crane safety, John put up a slide showing a photo of a number of different pieces of erection steel all in the same crane load, sticking out at weird angles. "Anyone in the room know what this is called?"

I waited. After a suitable amount of time where no one else answered, I replied. "That's called 'Christmas treeing.' It's illegal according to OSHA." I'd learned that one on the NJ road and bridge job.

John was impressed, in spite of himself. "That's right."

I finished the course. Then I had to be fingerprinted, pass a criminal background check, and have my work experience verified. NY City did not want unqualified people or those that might take bribes. When I took the four-hour site safety manager exam they checked my face against my driver's license photo, and finger-printed me again. It seemed that NY City did not want someone taking this critical exam in my place, either.

I finished the four-hour exam in 40 minutes. When walking up to turn in my answer sheet, I strolled past my classmates who couldn't seem to decide if I'd given give up or I was a genius.

Weeks later, when the results came back, I found I'd come close to a perfect score. I was in.

Life in the Big City

I was ready for them, but the NYC safety consulting firm was not ready for me. They had to wait for me to actually be issued the SSM license, or at least find me an opening that did not require one. During that time I took a short-term job auditing reseller telephone phone numbers for a large payphone company, saving them $8,000 a month from then on. But it was like a temp job I'd gotten for myself. I felt confined in an office. I longed to be out in the construction field, doing what I loved.

Then the safety firm, we'll call them Consulting Inc., called me in. They had a job for me but there was a problem. They'd asked the NJ construction firm for a reference. The New Jersey general contractor told them I was a horrible safety engineer, just the worst. The shortage was such that Consulting Inc. would hire me, but I would be on probation until I proved the NJ firm wrong.

I was sent to cover a New York City Department of Environmental Protection (DEP) job in lower Manhattan. This position did not technically require a site safety manager's license since the City would not write itself up for me not having one, and besides, my license was in process.

The project was demolition of a 125-year-old deteriorating facility that had been erected over the main water tunnel supplying NYC, something built directly over the tunnel before it burrowed under the East River bringing water to Brooklyn and Queens. Bricks had been falling off this structure, and the whole thing was swathed in protective netting until it was demolished. For over a century techs stationed there used to take water samples from a wide, deep well. The water tower, as they called it, was partially contaminated with mercury soaked into the concrete from decades of accidentally broken water testing instruments. The building was also rife with asbestos and lead, and it contained two ancient transformers right out of a Frankenstein movie full of carcinogenic PCBs.

The challenge was to take this facility down without contaminating the water for half of New York City.

51

Confessions of a Female Safety Engineer

Oh, and there was an elementary school right behind it. Try not to have anything fall on that, please? This was my first foray into NYC safety management, and the first job where I almost got killed.

OPERATION WATER SHIELD

THE DEP REP WOULD NOT LET ME SIT IN THEIR CONSTRUCTION TRAILER. The contractor did not want me in his, either. Again, this had nothing to do with me being a woman; the DEP guy was a lazy drone who didn't want people to see him playing solitaire on his computer almost all day, and the contractor resented the expense and scrutiny of any safety manager. They rented me a little guard booth, a sort of plastic office, something that looked like an ambitious port-a-john with windows, and was probably made by the same manufacturer. I was grateful it had a tiny table, a chair, and an electrical outlet. But I did not spend much time in my "office." I was outside, keeping an eye on the job.

The client's plan, once they were sure the 15-ft-wide circular well was stable, was to cover the well opening with multiple layers of thick planks and foam insulation, and then two layers of rolled neoprene roofing with thick glued seals, then several more layers of planking and foam insulation. This would keep the demolished materials from falling into the well. They called in some retired Navy Seals to look at the well; these men took one look at how deep it was and told them to get a robot, which they did. I was not involved in that part of the operation, but I saw the report. The deep sampling well walls were stable, so I handled the safety while they covered it.

Then we got rid of the contaminants in the building. We had an asbestos crew decontaminate the interior, and I dealt with all the insanity that entailed: the Federal, State, and City ordinances on asbestos removal are all different, and you had to know which regulation was the most stringent for each part of the operation and follow that one. I mainly checked the qualifications of the crew lead and let him handle it, and spot-checked his work to make sure he was not misrepresenting things in his reports. They did great. An independent asbestos lab certified from samples that the building was clean. Then I supervised the storage and shipment of the resulting hazardous asbestos waste: a legal minefield.

Confessions of a Female Safety Engineer

Next we decontaminated any areas in the structure with lead contamination. This mainly consisted of us removing lead-based paint in certain areas. To do that, you tent the space to keep the lead dust in, and sand blast the paint off. The lead waste was also stored and shipped properly.

The one floor where the instruments had leaked mercury onto the concrete was carefully broken up and removed as mercury hazardous waste. We actually caught a man trying to save money on shipping hazardous waste by picking out chunks of contaminated concrete out to throw away with the regular trash, with his bare hands. You could see the several cups of highly toxic mercury that he was pouring into a container. DEP went nuts and stopped him before I could. This was the guy who was my contact with our contractor client. His name was Fred, and in my mind I nicknamed him Freddy Mercury.

Con Edison, who tried to deny the ancient PCB-filled transformers were theirs, was forced to admit it when we showed them a photo of the plates bolted onto each of them. These plates read, in a typeface right out of a silent movie, "Property of the Consolidated Edison Company." We let Con Ed handle the environmental safety regarding the PCBs, a contaminant with which they unfortunately had a lot of experience dealing with. They swathed them in two layers of plastic and then lifted them out via a boom truck, through a window they removed, onto a flatbed truck that had a three-foot-high containment pan lined with more plastic. For the rest of my career, I was never so glad to see a truck leave one of my sites.

We took out the ancient elevator, which was quite a project in and of itself, and then installed temporary stairs. Then, the building demolition proper began.

The first step was to erect two sets of six-foot-tall wooden crash barriers between the building and the school which had a fence around their playground 300 feet away. Then my client used a crane to lift a remote-controlled robot demolition machine the size of a car to the roof. The robot's operator ran his controls from a safe location while the machine was out there where the roof might collapse. The robot could roll like a car, or waddle a walk like a dog, and instead of a head it had a jackhammer attachment. This jackhammer was four times the size of the ones you would see men using on a sidewalk. It took out everything between the roof beams. When it broke masonry, it was *loud*.

Everyone on the site had to wear earplugs and the robot's operator had to wear earplugs plus noise-cancelling earmuffs.

Do you know how people get used to overly-loud noises? By going deaf. Not on my site, if I could help it.

The next step was a team doing exploratory demotion of the walls from the inside of the top floor of the building. The team discovered that the support columns were spaced 32-feet apart—insanely wide—and that there were four courses of brick—two interior and two exterior.

Worst of all they discovered that there were no brick shelves to structurally hold these walls of brick up against gravity. Unreinforced masonry is not as big an issue in NY as it would be in places prone to earthquakes, but when it deteriorates it's a huge threat. The entire building was one great big sword of Damocles, hanging over the neighborhood.

So here is how they took that dangerous building down safely. Initial demolition of the upper floor walls was scheduled for a weekend, when school was out. They brought in a crane again; it held up a horizontal beam on a steel "Y" sling, and kept it level with the wall being removed. As the men on the top floors peeled off layers of bricks from the inside, sheets of unsupported bricks peeled off the exterior. These walls of brick were immense: they came loose in thirty-to-sixty-foot wide, 20-ft high double sheets. The thick sheet of bricks would bounce off the dangling beam that they held in front of it. It then fell almost straight down, and any splatter of bricks would hit the crash barriers. BOOM. Other than setting off all the car alarms in the neighborhood and a causing few erroneous bomb reports to the NYPD, no one was disturbed. We kept the concrete dust down with water spray, and shipped out the clean debris to a landfill.

Once we were sure that procedure would work, we did it during the week when school was open. The only variation was what we did if a part of the wall would not come loose from inside. We brought in a crane-suspended work platform, a cage that hung from the crane that the same demolition guys could climb into and access the wall from the outside. This was not a preferred method, as the suspended cage had no secondary backup if the hoisting cable failed. But the situation called for it, and I wrote up the safety documentation to back up the contractor for using that method.

Confessions of a Female Safety Engineer

At about this time, Freddy Mercury got tired of paying for me. They were using a huge onsite diesel generator for lights and power for the site and their offices, and to power things like the robot demolition machine. So to get rid of me, he intentionally aimed the diesel exhaust at the air vent for my office, and then ordered me to stay in that office for large swathes of time.

It was like a gas chamber. I couldn't breathe, which was his intention. I've never had asthma before or since, but I ended up with such a terrifying attack of reactive asthma to the diesel fumes that I left the site, desperately looking for medical help. I knew from what friends had told me that NYC hospitals were overburdened and you could die waiting to be seen in their emergency rooms, so I called my doctor and I was there and treated after frightening hour of not being able to breathe while driving.

Remember, these creeps knew I had kids, and I was a single parent, but they didn't care.

To make matters worse, I got a call from my supervisor, John, the guy who thought women should not be in the field. Remember, I was on probation. "Where the hell are you?" he fumed. But once he realized what they had done, and that I'd almost died, he took my side and gave 'em hell.

Diesel fumes bothered me for *years* after that incident.

Could I have sued the contractor? Probably. But I was on probation. I would have been kissing the career I'd worked so hard to get a quick goodbye if I went the lawyer route. So when John told me I'd been reassigned, I gratefully accepted the transfer while carrying an inhaler at all times.

Ironically, it was a job involving ventilation fans. And to qualify for it I needed more training. I needed New York City Transit track training, and a hands-on class on how to work on the NYC rails. They sent me to a training facility in Gravesend, Brooklyn, to learn the rules of working with NYCT.

Dodging Trains for Fun and Profit

This was in the days before **GPS** with cell phone navigation, so I bought a paper Hagstrom map book of NYC with detailed maps of all five boroughs, and left early in case I got lost. But the place was not too hard to find. The New York City Transit training facility was just off the Belt Parkway, in a WPA-era elementary school a few miles north of Coney Island. It had what I would learn to be an astonishing number of parking spaces for anything that deep into NYC.

First there was some book learning. OSHA regulations, and Federal Railroad Administration rules, did not always apply. This was New York City Transit, and their rules were more rigorous. We were given things to memorize like train signals, rules of the road, use of flagmen, proper safety gear to wear including a safety vest with break-way sides in case it snagged on a train. We learned how to "clear up" which meant picking a safe place to get out of the way of a train coming through. We learned that track switching locations were pinch points that could take off a foot, and that the third rail was so dangerous that if you touched it your dead body would be stuck via the current to the high-voltage line until the juice was turned off.

As always, I excelled in a classroom environment. But then the fun part came, the hands-on part that separated the men, as it were, from the boys. The whole class put on their safety gear and the instructor walked them a couple of blocks north to a train station. We all climbed down onto live tracks.

Now this was not just to see if you remembered your lessons, although there were some quizzes about what you learned. It was a test to see if you'd panic when your nose was inches from the outside of a moving train. Worse, they set it up so that you cleared up in between two concrete columns, with live tracks in front and behind you. And then they ran a train in front and another behind you, simultaneously. The one behind you was added without warning you in advance.

Now it was obvious they were running the trains as slowly as possible, and watching us like hawks to make sure we did not get hurt, but let's just say the resulting situation weeded out anyone who would panic. Years later, when I took a refresher, there were two other women in my class but not this time. As the only woman there I got special scrutiny.

After the trains had passed I put their minds at ease. I stretched and yawned and remarked dryly that I was now reconsidering that breast enlargement surgery. This was met with snorts of suppressed laughter from my classmates and the teacher.

I got my track training card and learned, as a safety manager, how to check for an expired or forged one.

Much of my career was spent in Transit work after that.

WEEKEND EXCURSIONS
AND VACATION RELIEF

IN BETWEEN ALL OF THE LONG-TERM PROJECTS I WAS ASSIGNED TO, THERE were little slices of this job or that, where I would spend anywhere from an evening to a month covering sick days, vacations and other absences for the other safety managers the consulting firm hired out. I was in demand because a site safety manager was required on large projects by New York City law. If there were no site safety manager on a job where one was required, the job could be fined and shut down for a minimum of two weeks. This was very expensive, because most jobs were on tight schedules and delays cost big money. And the delays were longer than the time you were shut down, because during that two weeks or more your tradesmen would start work on other sites and it was difficult to get them all back on *your* job, right away.

One of these short-term jobs was supposed to be a long-term one, but the contractor screwed up.

It was supposed to be a long-term hotel job for me in Manhattan's Chelsea neighborhood, just past a street of floral wholesalers, and not too far from the Fashion Institute of Technology (FIT).

I'd done half-face respirator fit testing at FIT for their maintenance staff, years ago when I was with the New England safety consulting firm. Back then, the specs said to use two types of testing—irritant smoke and banana oil--and I could only get the irritant smoke online or via mail order. The banana oil was actually considered "dangerous goods" and no one would ship it. There was no banana oil to be picked up in person within a day's drive, either. Since you only needed one test, I faked the banana oil by dropping by a bakery supply house and getting some banana flavoring, and I put it in a very official looking vial. The client was happy, and since they passed the irritant smoke testing their respirators fit properly.

The problem at the new site was that I was there three days when the Building Department came and was concerned about structural changes on the roof. The contractor had added something not on the plans to the building, a penthouse. The NYC Building Department gets copies of all structural blueprints before a job even starts. And the NYC construction inspectors, the Building Enforcement Safety Team affectionately known as the BEST Squad, noticed the additional penthouse. Where were the approved plans for it? And why hadn't they gotten them?

They wanted to see PE drawings. Now, I'd just been on the site a few days, so they were not upset with *me*. And using my newness on the site I admitted I had no idea where they kept things like sketches with a stamp from a licensed professional engineer, which was all that would save this contractor. I told the inspectors I assumed that such things were kept in the contractor's main office, I managed to negotiate that they come back for them tomorrow or we could have them to the Building Department by tomorrow, thereby buying the contractor time to have a rush job made of the PE drawings if they did not exist.

The BEST Squad inspectors were mollified, and were about to leave, when they ran into one of Consulting, Inc.'s supervisors. Now I have no idea what the guy who would have been my immediate supervisor on this site said to the BEST Squad guys, but by the time he was done they padlocked the site gate and put up a notice that the job was temporarily shut down. *Way to go, boss man!* I never did get my new printer back that was locked inside that site, but the boss paid for me to get a new one.

That was the only project I was ever on that was shut down while I was on the site. I was relocated, but the general contractor was out of luck.

Early in my NYC consulting I spent a couple weeks on and off at 2 Broadway, the Metropolitan Transit Authority's nearly-completed headquarters. At first I spent weekends there checking a crew's fall protection gear before they went into elevator shafts to paint, and then waiting around until they got out of those shafts confirming when they went home. Talk about boring! But I had the Statue of Liberty outside my window and brought in books to read. It sure beat my port-a-john office at the DEP water tower site!

Later, they brought me back to keep an eye on the MTA headquarters building when it was closer to completion. One of the things they were doing at this point was adding strength to a number of structural columns at this building's base. There had been so many changes to the original design on the floors above it that the architects structural engineer decided that certain columns which were already encased in sheetrock needed to be opened up and made stronger. These columns stood in completed rooms with finishes like carpets and furniture.

The welding required meant the finished room around the hot work had to be protected with fireproof tarps. When I came to these areas, I had to check that the tarps were adequate, and that the fellow who was on fire watch had his training card from the fire department and a working fire extinguisher. The person on fire watch was supposed to have construction's most widely used type of fire extinguisher, one that contained a multipurpose dry chemical propelled by a non-combustible gas that was effective on Class A, B, and C fires (everything except burning metals, and yes, some metals can burn). The powder in it creates a barrier between oxygen the fuel in a fire.

I found that one laborer on fire watch had the proper training card, but the pressure in his extinguisher was on empty. So I stopped the work while he went to get another extinguisher, but that one as empty, too. Then he had a bright idea. "Let me teach you an old Indian trick," he said with the confidence of a wise, old teacher. "It's just out of air; there is still a lot of that powder in there."

I did not interrupt him, yet. I was rather fascinated with his mansplaining to me how he was going to get around the need for a commercial fire extinguisher company to recharge it.

"So all ya gotta do is put some more air in." He proceeded to take the extinguisher over to a compressed gas tank to refill it with "air."

He was going to fill it with oxygen! *Oxygen* to fill up a fire extinguisher! Dear God.

It took me several tries to get it across to him what a really bad idea that was. The thing that finally broke through his ignorance was when I said, "Remember the space shuttle Challenger, when it exploded?" I simplified it for him. "That was because the oxygen in it caught on fire."

"Holy sh*t!" the guy exclaimed. Um, yeah.

This fellow was representative of one of three main groups who work in construction. First there are those who are attracted to the problem-solving and technical aspects of building or demolishing things: such as architects who solve design problems, engineers who solve mathematical problems, project managers and those who solve implementation problems, and folks like me and field engineers who do a little of all that. The second main group of people in construction are skilled artisans or craftsmen who love to work with their hands: jobs like finish carpenters, electricians, stone masons, plumbers, even those who paint or install windows.

And finally, there is a third group: those who end up in construction since they can't find a job anywhere else. Most of those people get into the rhythm of the work and do fantastic jobs. Some, not so much. I had to deal workers who's do things like insulate high-pressure steam pipes before they were welded together, or guys who would store clear poison solvents in a lemon-lime soft drink bottle. A great deal of my work in heavy construction safety consisted in protecting people like the man who wanted to fill the fire extinguisher with oxygen from *themselves*, and protecting their co-workers from such stupidity. These workers would do things like wear a fall protection harness attached to a 20-ft rope on a 10-ft roof, and not see what the problem was (true story).

Many of the short-term projects were night work or NYC Transit station or track closings, or on "General Orders," colloquially known as GOs. GOs were usually 52-hour subway or elevated railway weekend station closings, from late Friday night to very early Monday mornings. There was *always* a station being repaired. The work was endless, and occasionally I worked a double or triple shift on a closed station; they were so short of people with my credentials that they'd beg me to stay and sleep the third shift in my car, just so long as I was there and they could wake me if an inspector came. The only reason I did not work GOs almost every weekend was that my two remaining teen sons and I were helping take care of my elderly mother. The boss was really good about allowing me time for that.

I'll tell you about any other strange ways I spent my weekends but always assume that if I had overtime, it was on a transit job in the evening or on a weekend. The only thing rarer than a licensed NYC site safety manager was one with NYC track training. I did not have to worry about unemployment, to say the least

Not all of the fill-in work was on transit sites though. There were night shifts during start up testing at the new Con Ed plant in Astoria, Queens. There were commercial buildings, hospitals, residential high rises, hotels, factories, and schools that could only bring in a crane for things like replacing HVAC equipment on their roof on the weekends. Oh, the insanity of DOT (NYC Department of Transportation) permits for crane work was only surpassed by the NYC Cranes & Derricks paperwork for getting a crane on site. All of this work had to be pre-planned in advance, and I often did that safety preplanning work, too.

Some of the small jobs were a thrill a minute, sometimes they were grueling, but more often such fill-in work was extremely boring. Perhaps my favorite of those slow ones was a day I spent on a rush job putting a new kitchen into an upscale midtown Hilton. The plumbers and electricians were working three shifts, including weekends, to get that new kitchen up and running as soon as possible. One Saturday was I called in for a full eight-hour day to do intermittent safety inspections on some very safe, end-of-project work. Since the safety office was closed for the weekend, the client asked me to wait in between inspections in the employee dining area, which was still running.

What a luxurious day! I had chefs trying to tempt me and bringing me fresh coffee or treats while I read a book or did crosswords in between safety checks that took no more time than a bathroom break. I had wonderful conversations with their security staff, telling me about the time Clint Eastwood helped them break up a fight. But the chefs had no idea who I was.

After about five hours of this, one of the chefs came out on his way home, full of sympathy that "the person I had waited for all day" had never shown up. He'd made me a little cheesecake in the shape of a four-leaf clover, for luck. I explained why I was there and assured him I was getting paid to sit here most of the day, and they'd made my day the gastronomic experience of a lifetime.

There were short-term jobs for me until longer-term ones opened up, too. One project was to put handicap-friendly elevators on a subway station in mid-Queens. That job had the distinction of me finding a way to keep the buses from ruining part of their work. They had just demolished a concrete curb and re-poured a concrete ramp leading to the handicap elevator at the street level. The problem, as I saw it, was that tire tracks told me that the frequent NYC transit busses routinely ran over that curb. How could we be absolutely certain the busses would not ruin the wet cement?

Now that was not life and limb safety matter, but it was still part of my job: property damage is something we safety managers try very hard to avoid.

Confessions of a Female Safety Engineer

And when you want to get someone to do something, you find out what would motivate them that is in their interests. So banged on the passenger door of one bus stopped at the light near the new concrete. I was wearing a Transit safety vest, and the white hardhat and clipboard said "management," so the driver opened up the bus door.

"Yes?" said the driver.

I pointed. "They just poured fresh concrete there. It's going to be a hazard for the busses since they might get stuck in it. Can you radio your dispatcher and have him warn everyone who drives a bus on this line?"

He sure could call his dispatcher, and he thanked me profusely for the warning. Not a single bus strayed and damaged the concrete so it dried intact.

Another short-term job was vacation relief for a project where a Chinese company was building a window factory in northern Queens, off the Whitestone Expressway. This one only had one worker who spoke English. He translated the safety training but he was rarely there. Everything else was communicated to the workers like a game of Pictionary: we'd draw pictures back and forth to each other until we understood each other. It worked surprisingly well.

Related was a short-term job near the entrance to the Holland Tunnel, where another Chinese firm was going to build a hotel. The Chinese loathe unions, and they had set up their own network of construction finance, supply and tradesmen to get around them. But that did not exempt them from being scrutinized by the NYC Department of Buildings, or OSHA. In fact, the Chinese hotel job in lower Manhattan was a block from OSHA's regional office, and they might send out inspectors to us as a training exercise at any time. Had they done so, let's just say that OSHA would not have been able to read the safety training that the foremen had translated into Chinese for me to share with the men, or signatures, at least not without a translator.

The Chinese hotel job was at the excavation stage, and it was the first project I was on that required the underpinning of an adjacent building. Underpinning is a way of adding a foundation or strengthening a foundation below ground level to support or strengthen the building above it. It's extremely tricky and requires a sketch and calculations from a licensed professional engineer, known as PE drawings. These PE drawings had to be submitted to the building department in advance, for approval. So you can just bet the

64

Wendy S. Delmater

building department would show up and make sure they were followed to the letter: if done incorrectly, the building being underpinned could collapse.

And it was a very good thing the BEST Squad were there. They witnessed the correct underpinning being done and pretty much signed off on the work. The adjacent 12-story building owner's attempt to extort money out of the company running the construction--for what turned out to be preexisting or nonexistent damage--was thwarted by the City of NY itself, later, in court.

But the Chinese crew did not do the underpinning; a specialty crew did that. Then it got cold. The Chinese crew doing the hotel foundation still had no trailer to warm up in and it was the dead of winter. They spoke no English, but loved me because they I let them pack into my warm car and thaw out as needed (as long as they did not smoke in my car; they all smoked like chimneys). When I left, they presented me with a huge bag of jasmine tea as a gift.

I got to bring that and some fascinating stories home to the dinner table.

Sometimes you wanted a building to come down. Demolition was often done over the weekend, too, when there were fewer people in NYC. Demo is one of the last things you learn to do as a trainee safety manager, since it's one of the most dangerous. The worst of those were when a building was being remodeled: demo companies often destroyed expensive things that were carefully marked to be left alone. Unless you watched them they always wantonly broke things (a form of property damage), like fire protection panels, plumbing or wiring, causing great delays and expense. Demolition detail was not my favorite work.

After the water tower job, the safety consulting firm felt I could handle demolition and I oversaw part of the tear down of the building behind the Time Square ball drop site. I did that for a few days until a long-term transit job in the Bowery started.

FAN DANCE

FRESH AIR HAD TO GET INTO THE SUBWAY TUNNELS SOMEHOW, AND THIS WAS one of the places that pumped it in. The project involved adding a lower chamber to a fan room, and two more huge ventilation fans like you'd expect were used testing airplane designs in wind tunnels. The work was under a street, and every day that street was opened by removing steel plates with thick pavement and recessed lift points on top, using an excavator bucket, with hooks and chains.

My introduction to the site was pretty weird. I found it on my Hagstrom map, and drove in early to find a parking spot. Once I was parked, I decided to use the site's port-a-john. As I was about to leave the little jobsite toilet, someone started banging angrily on the door, growling loudly and cursing up a storm.

I peered out cautiously.

A older man in construction gear backed away, blushing and looking surprised. "Oh my God! I'm sorry! I thought you were one of the homeless guys!"

I just started at him.

"The Bowery Mission is right up the street, you know, and we get a lot of homeless bums. Sorry. Who are you?"

I stepped out, and dusted my slacks off. "I'm your new safety manager."

The guy was the operator of the backhoe that opened and closed the street every day, and lowered down materials into the excavation. He would become my fiercest defender when the sad fellows who overflowed from the Mission aggressively panhandled in my vicinity. I asked him where the site office was, and he showed me.

Well, that office was different. Site management was housed in what used to be a cold storage facility. The rooms had thick, thick white plaster walls, all curved like an ice cave. The building was on the edge of the trendy East Village, and every ice cave but ours had been converted into one of a warren of artists' studios. Later in the project we were working on a Saturday (a crane was finally bringing in the new fans) when the artists ran an open house. I was in the elevator, dressed in khakis, a polo shirt, construction boots, a NYC Transit safety vest, and a hard hat. The rest of the elevator was full of people touring the artist's studios. "And what are you?" one of them asked me.

I told them I was performance art. And they believed me.

There were a lot of weird things about that neighborhood. It was on the edges of the Bowery, Chinatown, and the East Village, across from a park you would not could walk through at night because of the addicts, and right off of trendy Houston (which New Yorkers pronounce *Howes-ton*) Street. There were night clubs, cheap eats, upscale restaurants, vintage clothing stores, an indie movie theater, overspill from NYU...and the lobby of the weird building our office was housed in became a bazaar where unwanted art or odd furniture was given away. I brought home all sorts of free things.

In that office I started a trend that followed me throughout my career, of getting a great reputation simply because the person I was replacing was incompetent. I suppose that was in part because of the shortage of site safety managers so they weren't being too careful about who they hired—but the fact that employers would try almost anyone as a SSM meant they at least gave me a chance, so that was fine with me. At this project, at least, I think the contrast between me and the previous safety manager who kept writing his own customer up and lived only in the office was good for my image.

But I was rarely in that office. Outside was dangerous work that required constant vigilance.

Our excavation took us very close to some underground high voltage lines, and we cracked one of the concrete sections that covered them with the metal excavator bucket. Very scary work. There are so many underground utilities in NYC, and many times they are not clearly marked.

You see, during the blizzard of 1888, a recently electrified NYC underwent a massive storm that tore down all of its power lines from the weight of the snow: 20.9 inches with 30-ft drifts. When the utilities were rebuilt, rather than re-establish electrical poles the City made the decision to mandate that utilities put as much of their infrastructure underground as they could. So underground utilities were everywhere. I ran into a lot of underground issues on my career. It was not just electrical conduits—there were gas and steam lines, and communications wires, too—but electrical conduits were a main reason I would call for utility "mark outs" before my men excavated.

Speaking of utilities, perhaps the scariest thing that happened near this site was a Con Ed gas leak. I reported it, and they showed up but could not find it, so Con Ed left. Soon after that, I could suddenly smell it again while we were doing "hot work" which is work with open flames. That was alarming. I stopped the work and directed the men to set up a water spray to cool things down until Con Ed came back. They smelled the leaking natural gas this time, and shut off the gas line to excavate. They had to replace a 30-ft section of eight-inch natural gas pipe that had rusted pretty much through. Had that gas caught a spark from our hot work and exploded, it would have taken out an entire city block.

But for me, that was just life in the big city.

THE VIEW FROM
NINE CIRCUIT BREAKER HOUSES

CONSULTING INC. NEXT ASSIGNED ME TO JOB WITH A CLIENT WHO HAD transit work all over the city. This project was to replace several circuit breaker houses on multiple subway lines in Brooklyn, Queens and the Bronx – mostly in Queens, so that's where it was based. It had a lot of electricians who wanted to skip lunch and go home early to avoid the traffic. That would mean great hours for me since at the time I needed to get my elderly mother to dialysis three evenings a week. My youngest son was a senior in high school; he and my middle son, my sister and I were taking care of mom.

Finding the office for this job was hard. At the address I was given there was a run-down liquor store. I passed it several times, disbelieving, but finally went it. It turned out that that *was* the office: the liquor store had closed. They were renting it out until they could find something better, and they had. We'd move someplace nicer tomorrow. I was warned not to put any of my things on the floor. The place was crawling with insects. Gah. That evening, I laid Combat roach disks all around our apartment to make sure I had not brought any home.

The next day, we moved the site office. The new location was certainly cleaner but it was, in its own way, even more disreputable. We were on the second floor, above the most physically clean porno shop you could imagine. Every day as I went up to the office, I noted they were cleaning the shop downstairs. They obsessively washed the windows, scrubbed the floors, and polished their counters. "Does having a sparkling clean *porn* shop strike anyone else as ironic?" I asked my co-workers. They shrugged.

It was a great management team to work with. The first part of their project right was outside our door, on the #7 train line at Courthouse Square station. There were also two other retrofit circuit breaker houses locations running simultaneously, where I delegated the safety and traveled to inspect them. But the one outside our office was a new circuit breaker house, and the weight of it required more structural steel underneath, so that's where I spent most of my time.

Confessions of a Female Safety Engineer

It was an interesting neighborhood. It had a literal school for graffiti artists, who contracted out their services for murals and decked their building with new designs every week. There were multiple inexpensive places to eat, and one block over there was a facility that stocked the coffee and pastry carts all over NYC. The man who stocked these licensed food carts rented them out; licenses were very expensive, rather like taxi medallions. At the end of the day the people who rented the carts would return them after throwing out their unsold inventory. If you asked, they'd just give free food to you. I'd bring my sons home buttered rolls and muffins, donuts, and Danish. Since we could only eat so many of them, I brought home as much as the local emergency food pantry at my church could handle.

Every time I got on or off the overhead rail for the #7 train at Courthouse Square Station to inspect the other sites, I noted the station actually *swayed* when the trains came in. That struck me as odd. And the swaying of the station got worse as the months progressed. It was swaying an entire foot. I wondered why.

For a while, the circuit breaker house outside our office was the only one being worked on, a not-yet energized structure that a couple of electricians entered to do wiring in. Not much to watch, as it was very safe work, but I was required by law to be there. So I filled my time by reading the job specifications, and used those to make sure we had all the MSDS sheets for the job. And through a combination of reading those specs, and field observations, I discovered the terrifying reason why Courthouse Square Station was swaying.

The new circuit breaker house just past the Courthouse Square Station needed structural reinforcement underneath. The original steel columns dated from the era of Charlie Chaplin. They already had stiffening plates; our ironworkers were to add another plate on each side of each column. The specifications stated that the ironworkers that were "sistering up" (splinting, reinforcing) the steel columns under it were only supposed to pop out two to three rivets at a time, replacing them with torqued bolts. Instead, they were popping six or eight rivets at a time. And the steel plate was *bowing*, bending in an arc due to sideways stresses on the column.

Now I'm no structural engineer, but that was just wrong. It shouldn't be doing that. So I called the project manager down to take a look at it, and he called in the architect's structural engineer. She—an iron-haired matron

Wendy S. Delmater

PhD from the Ukraine—saw the bowing and almost passed out from shock. She ordered immediate blocking: heavy timbers stacked to take the column's weight.

When they excavated to the base of the column, they discovered that an underground stream had washed away its foundation, and this column, the one that took all the stresses on this curved section of overhead track was about to fail. That was what was causing Courthouse Square Station to sway; the whole section of track and the station were about to fall on busy Jackson Avenue, NY Route 25A. I was a hero to NYC Transit, and to my consulting client who got paid for a great big fat change order for the extra emergency work.

However my supervisor at the consulting company, John, was furious with me. They'd been on a legal language kick at Consulting Inc. and he was all worried about the company being sued. "What do you think you're doing? You're not a structural engineer! You had no business saying anything. What's wrong with you?"

Oh yes, I had just about had it with John. I complained to one of Consulting, Inc.'s other supervisors, we'll call him Terry, who was sympathetic. That became important later on.

My Bird's-Eye-View of 9/11

I WAS STILL AT THE CIRCUIT BREAKERS HOUSES JOB. AT 9 AM ON SEPTEMBER 11, 2001, I was supposed to be at their job progress meeting at NYC Transit headquarters, which was the same 2 Broadway I'd worked at in lower Manhattan, but the meeting was postponed. So I was on the #7 train, coming back to the office from looking at one of our remote circuit breaker house retrofits. The train was on the elevated section of track that ran in the middle of Queens Boulevard, a main route into Manhattan heading toward the Queensboro Bridge. I was looking out the window past Aviation High School when I first noticed flames coming out of one of the distant twin towers.

"Wow," I remarked to a fellow passenger, "there's a fire at the World Trade Center."

A lady across the aisle, next to the conductor's booth, said, "Yes, the conductor just heard about it on his radio. A plane hit it."

"That's terrible," the man next to me said, shaking his head. We all watched the fire through the train windows until the view was obscured by a building, and then I got off at the (no longer swaying) Court Square Station.

I came down the stairs from the station to find the sidewalk filled with people, all looking toward the twin towers, which were due west down the street, direct line-of-sight. My project manager was among them. "I saw the other plane hit," he informed me, and like everyone else who got that news I realized we were under attack.

If you were in New York City that morning you couldn't watch TV coverage of the disaster, and you could not hear about it on the radio. All of our local broadcast towers were atop those burning structures, coming down when they did. But a local business had the BBC network on cable, and I watched the agonizing pictures of jumpers and falling rubble from there. I'd been scheduled to be two blocks from the towers; I'd have been at that postponed meeting at 8:30 AM. The pictures of people running from the falling rubble and women emerging from clouds of white concrete dust, coated and terrified, hit me

75

especially hard. That could have been me, had the scheduled meeting actually happened.

The word was to just get home, so I walked to the E subway to take the train, but the trains were not running. On my way back to the site office I pushed through crowds of panicked people in the street, darting to and fro like schools of fish avoiding a predator, terrified of any planes in the air if the plane strayed near the nearby Citibank building, the tallest building in Queens. What if a plane hit that, too?

One of my coworkers who'd brought his car in drove me as far as a Long Island Railroad station, and dropped me off there. After the NYPD went through the train cars with bomb sniffing dogs, we were told we did not need a ticket; just get in and get home. It was obviously something they'd drilled for; they were following an emergency contingency plan.

I took my car home from my local commuter rail station, and like everyone else in America who was not a first responder to the three locations in NY, PA and DC, I huddled near the light of our collective television news, fending off the dark.

Working in the City, I realized, was about to get very different.

RECONNAISSANCE

THE DAY AFTER 9/11, I WAS WORRIED ABOUT MY SITES. ALL THE KIDS IN NYC were not in school and we'd shut up the multi-location project so quickly that it might not be safe for them, perhaps making what insurance companies called an "attractive nuisance," some place children might explore and get hurt.

So the next morning after the 9/11 attacks, I decided to head back into NYC and make sure our construction sites were secure. Problem was, the trains were not running and the bridges into Manhattan, where one of the sites was, would only allow you across if there were four people in your vehicle.

I drove in, checked the Queens sites, and as I got near Manhattan I picked up three harmless people at bus stops who were waiting for busses that would never come. That got us all across a bridge into Manhattan. I dropped my passengers off at or near their jobs in Manhattan, and checked that our closed midtown site was secured. Then, on a whim, I went to the Javits Center where they were organizing the 9/11 rescue volunteers and supplies that were pouring in.

My boss was the head of the NY Metro chapter of the ASSE, and members of ASSE across the country would no doubt be funneling their relief efforts through him. I got a list of the rescue volunteers' safety needs from their organizers, plus info on where to deliver it. Since cell phones were still not working—their transmitters had been on the Towers, too—I asked a local store to use their land line to call my boss with the list.

The closest business was a liquor store. Sure I could use their phone. Did I want any booze? They insisted I take one of their lunches. That was the mood in NYC after the 9/11 attacks: everyone wanted to help. Under the crust New Yorkers have to develop to live in such close quarters, they are some of the most generous people in the world. One of the few positives after the 9/11 attacks was that everyone got to see that heartwarming side of the City.

I was able to reach my boss. He put me on speakerphone; they'd been calling NYC's Emergency Management Office for advice all day, but—as we'd later learn—that office had been destroyed with the Towers so there had been no answer. Supplies were indeed funneling through him as the local ASSE chapter president, headed toward NYC from around the country: respirators, safety shoes, safety glasses, and more. My list of the 9/11 volunteer coordinator's needs was received with alacrity, as was the information as to where to send it. Since no one could not reach the already-dispatched supply trucks, I was asked to stand watch with another site safety manager, to redirect the trucks from their interim destination—our main office in Queens—to the loading dock at the Javits Center. My co workers and I took turns on watch until all the trucks were in.

⚠

My work environment changed dramatically after 9/11. Understand that there was still plenty of infrastructure work that needed repaired, and these contracts had been put out to bid years ago, so the work certainly did not stop after 9/11. But the tenor changed. I changed.

On a personal level, after a series of indelible nightmares about terrorist bombings, I developed an irrational fear of taking tunnels under the rivers. On a professional level, doing emergency evacuation plans and drills became much more important.

My focus at the time was a replacement circuit breaker house just off the Queensboro Plaza station, one the last station above Queens Blvd. before the elevated train lines went into tunnels under the East River and into Manhattan. The circuit breaker house we were working on in was in a pretty rough neighborhood full of "Gentlemen's Clubs," flashers, and prostitution, but the post 9/11 security checkpoint made it one of the safest places in the city. If I had to work a triple shift and napped in my car, I napped unafraid.

When I had to work in the #7 train tunnel under the East River during GOs, it was always with the knowledge that there were security cameras on me, making sure I was not a terrorist about to blow the tunnel up.

NYC Transit had always done contractor safety seminars. Now they added a series of anti-terrorism seminars, and I learned far more about how we were at risk than I was comfortable knowing.

Wendy S. Delmater

It was a month after the 9/11 attacks. One evening I was called into a job in Manhattan, which was cancelled, so I went home early. I was on the #7 train, taking it to a station where I could switch to the Long Island Railroad, and home.

Across the subway car from me was a man in a red, white, and blue security uniform. He was obviously in shock. I asked him if he was okay. He looked up, eyes haunted, and said, "I just found out about the Towers."

No need to ask which Towers. But – a month later? "Where the hell have you been?"

The man been on vacation for the last month, on an island off the Great Barrier Reef in Australia, with no television or internet. His flight back from Australia had gotten in during the wee hours of the morning, and he'd dressed and headed into his work as a security guard for Cantor Fitzgerald. He could not take his usual train the whole way there, so he walked. As he got to Canal Street, he saw police all over the place and wondered why they were there. A few blocks closer to his job, he started to see army vehicles, which alarmed him. And then he walked around a corner and he could suddenly see that the World Trade Center towers were gone; just a smoking hole in the ground remained.

He sat heavily on the steps of a building.

A soldier came over to check on him. "Are you okay?"

"They're gone. The Towers are gone!"

The soldier looked at him funny. "Where the hell have you been?"

The soldier had him taken to the Javits Center, where they were still making up a list of the dead and missing. The man had spent all day there, being questioned, filling out forms, and basically reacting the way the rest of America did when they first found out. He discovered that all of his co-workers—all of them—had died in the attacks.

I suggested, gently, that he could apply for unemployment. He looked up, distressed and distracted, and admitted he'd not thought of that. There may have been scam artists trying to cash in on 9/11 but this was not one of them. I saw on his face what we all must have looked like on that fateful day. Shock. Horror. Numbness. He was a stranger but I gave him a hug, knowing it would not even dent his pain.

We were all changed on that day. He just got the memo a little later than we did.

Confessions of a Female Safety Engineer

⚠️

Meanwhile, I was still on the long-term Transit project. We finished a couple of circuit breaker houses in the Bronx, one circuit breaker house on an elevated railway in a Korean neighborhood, and one in northern Queens at the station closest to LaGuardia Airport. This one was a retrofit of a space that had asbestos insulation to be abated from some wiring. I had to check not just everyone's track training, but their asbestos certifications as well. It was the first time I had to deny people the ability to work based on expired and/or forged credentials, which was sad. But I'd learned over the years that in a man's world you do not, as a sacred rule, threaten another man's livelihood, unless what he is doing threatens *your* livelihood. Then you can make an acceptable exception. If I allowed them to work with forged or expired credentials and I got caught, I could lose my SSM license, my job, and my livelihood.

They were disappointed but they understood. That was the unwritten code.

Near Grand Army Plaza

WHEN THE CIRCUIT BREAKER HOUSES JOB WAS OVER, THE RUINS OF THE TWO towers were still smoking in lower Manhattan. You could see it to the west from the roof of my new project in Park Slope, in Brooklyn. If you looked to the east you could just see the edge of the traffic circle around a triumphant arch commemorating the North's victory in the Civil War at Grand Army Plaza. The Brooklyn Museum was just past that, and a nice park south of it all: Prospect Park.

This was a high-end neighborhood of brownstone homes. Brownstones in NYC are a particular type of townhouse made with sandstone. If you've never been to the city you've probably seen brownstones in movies such as *Home Alone 2: Lost in NY*, or *Moonstruck*.

The soon-to-be 16-story apartment building on Union Street was half-finished, built on what used to be the back yard of a huge mansion. Those who lived in the condominium on the west side of the new building used to have windows that looked down onto a garden; now, residents on the east side of the building had lost their "light and air" rights and had a brick wall for a view. "Light and air" rights are a huge issue in all of New York City real estate law, and the nextdoor residents felt that the permits for the job had been rammed through without their being able to go to hearings and dispute them, or even ask for compensation. In effect, they were furious because they felt they'd been robbed.

So the site had problems with vandalism, especially with the DOT barriers that kept our parking lane free for things like cranes and deliver trucks.

This dispute predated my arrival at the site, but I was part of the enemy because I worked there. And our tightwad client who would not pay for a legally-required security guard for a 15-or-more-story construction project? Not helping.

One 30ish Asian woman resident of the neighboring building in particular kept moving the DOT barriers and parking her car there, screaming obscenities at us when we complained. She tore down all the job-made no-parking signs

Confessions of a Female Safety Engineer

down, too, and she tore down any of our permits we posted. I don't know how she moved the traffic barricades: they had heavy 12" by 12" timber bases with a six-foot orange and white fences with blinking traffic lights on each, but she got them, too. We'd even tried drilling holes through the timbers to pound rebar into the pavement so they wouldn't budge. But every day we would come in to find the barricades all shoved aside, and the entire closed-off DOT permit lane full of parked cars. I ordered semi-permanent metal DOT "Construction Zone: No Parking" signs that she could not tear down, but those had not been delivered yet.

Most days it did not matter, and the worst problem I had on that site was asking the burly ironworkers working on the upper floors to have their friendly wrestling matches off the site, or at least where I could not see them. But when we had deliveries, the cars packed in the lane we were supposed to have control of made life hell. The client's project manager refused to tow the illegally-parked cars, even for deliveries. Yet he insisted that the deliveries go forward. His solution was to put a flagman on either end of the block and essentially turn one of the busiest two-way through streets in Brooklyn into a one way street with intermittent closures on each end, *without the necessary DOT permits.* He was taking an enormous legal risk, and remember, I could not write up my client. I called my boss in exasperation to try and get him to talk sense into this contractor. But nothing worked.

What this contractor did not know was that the head of the city's Department Of Transportation, Iris Weinshall—I believe she was married to US Senator Charles Schumer—lived right up the street. When her limousine was delayed by my client's illegal lane closure she checked and discovered that he did not have the requisite permits. She dragged the owner of the contracting company into her main DOT offices and screamed that if she EVER caught them doing something like that again they would never get another DOT permit until the day they *died*. That would, effectively, mean they would not be able to work in NYC ever again.

And yet, the next time there was to be a delivery, Super Sailor Moon had moved the barricades and her car was parked in our area. The project manager still refused to tow it. My solution was to call down a dozen iron workers, issue them new gloves so they would not scratch her paint, and politely ask them to pick up her little car, and move it ten feet to an empty parking spot outside of our lane closure. Challenge accepted!

They had donned the gloves and were about lift her car when she came screeching out of her building, furious that we would touch her illegally parked car. She called the police to report our outrageous behavior. A nice black NYPD cop showed up almost immediately. She listened to the venom-spitting harpy, then listened to my quiet explanation. Then she looked at the car and the permits and the construction barricades.

The cop turned to Super Sailor Moon and in an authoritative voice, she said simply, "Lady, move your damned car." Our tormentor turned red with fury, but moved her car and never bothered us again.

It probably helped that the next time a BEST Squad inspection rolled around, the Building Department inspector, who was a friend of mine, insisted that the contractor get a security guard. That inspector may or may not have gotten a hot tip that the contractor was not following the NYC construction law which required a security guard for a 15-story or taller project.

whistles innocently

Send in the Clowns

Not all of the work was scary. Some of it was absurd.

For example, try to imagine a job progress meeting for a $200 million dollar job. There's a complex of six construction trailers all connected for the general contractor. Its conference room is lined with cheap faux wood paneling, there are file cabinets full of engineering paperwork along one wall. There's a hanging rack of blueprints in the corner. Two walls are covered with white boards covered with scrawled engineering sketches and schedule items.

The people around this table are all project managers, lead superintendents, subcontractor owners, and project engineers, each handling work worth tens of millions of dollars.

And in the center of that table are two men wearing yellow hard hats with black stripes done in electrician's tape, striped like yellow jacket wasps. Both hard hats have insect antennas on top. The men wearing them are deathly serious. Well, at least the senior of the two men is serious, his subordinate is trying for a serious expression but looks a little embarrassed. And the lead electrician, from under his silly hat, intones in sepulchral seriousness, "We're protesting the bees."

How did we get to this point?

The electrician's superintendent on this site had been difficult, to say the least. And he had a reputation: when other trades heard this man would be the running this job, some of them withdrew their bids.

This electrical super always had an axe to grind, a complaint, a grievance. The general contractor would deal with one of his problems, and he'd promptly come up with another. His most recent grievance was that two Mondays ago one of his apprentice electricians had reached into her cargo box and discovered the hard way that some bees had made a nest in her metal tool chest over the weekend. As safety manager, after last week's meeting I'd issued a directive for all trades to check their cargo boxes before putting their hands in them,

Confessions of a Female Safety Engineer

and disseminated a sales circular on where to buy wasp killer spray. The lead electrician was not satisfied.

This led to a little meeting in my office with my project manager. Our decision, since the lead electrician would just find a new problem when we solved this one, was that we should ride the "issue" with the bees as far as we could.

During the job progress meeting we all treated our antennaed electrician superintendent's problem as serious and no one cracked a smile. As soon as he left and the door was closed, however...we all laughed until we cried. The project manager and I wiped our tears and he admitted, "I think we've run this as far as we can."

No argument there. But how to mollify the ridiculous man about his "bee problem"?

There were yellow jackets swirling above a 40-yard dumpster that took the trash from all of the trades' construction trailers, a dumpster which was parked in front of the electrician's office. The electrical super was satisfied we had done or duty when we had it moved across the street.

And, sure enough, he immediately found something else to complain about.

⚠

On one of my sites, the weekly job progress meeting had a shop steward instead of a superintendent to represent his trade. We suspected he was only there for the free bagels and coffee, and to rest while getting paid for an hour, but we tolerated it. And to his credit, he really tried to bring a safety concern to every meeting. The problem was, the job was so safe he started to have difficulty finding any problems to bring up at all.

One week, the best "safety concern" the shop steward could come up with was to ask us to look into a strong paint or solvent smell that had happened in a particular location – three days ago.

"Three days ago?" I said. "Why didn't you let us know about it when it happened? How can we fix it now?" I paused, and then decided to use an analogy. "When a puppy pees on the floor, you don't wait three days to rub it's

86

nose into it. You do it right away, and slap the puppy so it knows it was wrong."

The room, including the embarrassed shop steward, roared with laughter for a couple of minutes. When the hilarity died down an engineer went up and wrote "Slap the puppy" on the whiteboard, and they all lost it again.

"Slap the puppy" became our slogan on that site. The shop steward still came to the meetings, and got his bagel, but he made no more silly requests.

⚠

Sometimes, you, the safety manager, can be the clown.

Often, I would walk into a room of men, and all talk would cease. I'd ask what was wrong, and they'd say something along the lines of, "Oh, what we were talking about was off-color and we thought you might not like it. " While I appreciated the sentiment, I also needed to get them to treat me as an equal. My standard response in such situations was to smile and say, *That's nice. But just remember I have three kids* and *I did not get them through artificial insemination*. Things usually thawed after the guffaws died down.

On one of my projects, the carpentry subcontractor went out of business, and the general contractor took on all of his workers as their own employees. This required a mass-orientation of over a hundred men. It was early in my safety career and I needed to set my posture with these men, quickly and effectively. But how to do so?

After giving them a "here's what your new employer wants from you regarding safety" speech, I let them know that I'd been married to a carpenter so I knew all of their tricks, and all of their jokes. I then proceeded to give some rapid-fire punch lines to some of the rowdiest, most off-color jokes I knew. Not the jokes themselves, just the punch lines. You'd have to know the jokes themselves to realize what these phrases referred to. Half the carpenters in the room recoiled in respectful shock; the other half asked their friends what I meant and were shushed and told, "I'll tell you later." I had no trouble with that crew after that.

ON THE FLYING TRAPEZE

I WAS NEXT POSTED AT A RESIDENTIAL TOWER PROJECT THAT THEY WERE building on the Lower West Side of Manhattan, where the multi-lane West Side Hwy becomes one-lane West Street. While I was there, it was the first Fleet Week after 9/11. Fleet Week is a big celebration in New York City, unofficially dating back to the Spanish-American War but officially a Thing since 1988. I had a bird's eye view from my project. There were ships from the US and a number of countries, and as they passed lower Manhattan all hands were on deck, in dress uniforms, saluting NYC. To add to the colorful ambiance, there was an outdoor trapeze school across the street. Even the trapeze students stopped to watch the ships pass.

The project I was working on had fall protection issues, too, and unlike the trapeze students they were working without a net. I explained to them that the scaffold on the roof had inadequate guardrails and they fixed it right away.

Scaffolds. One of the most troubling things safety managers have to deal with is scaffolding. If we can avoid using a scaffold, we try to do so. One safety manager I know used nothing but scissor lifts on his site to avoid them. Another site avoided a mason's scaffold by the brick walls on that skyscraper being made in sections on the ground; they had the finished sections of walls lifted into place and attached to the structural steel by ironworkers. I'd often suggest a secured ladder, instead, to get the fall protection issues to under OSHA's ladder standard instead of their scaffolding regulations.

Because scaffolds were a pain in the rear. Take mason's tube & coupler steel scaffolds, for example. They're a safety nightmare to install, a safety nightmare to maintain, and a safety nightmare to disassemble. If they are on upper floors they have to be tied into the building for structural integrity, and you need a PE drawing for that. Such scaffolds also have maintenance issues like making sure the platform boards do not split or crack, and that the safety railings are maintained.

And guess who had to go out there and climb all over large scaffold systems to make sure they were in good shape? The safety manager. I cannot tell you how many scaffolds I inspected over the years: hanging scaffolds, pump jack scaffolds, cantilevered scaffolds, mobile scaffolds for interior use, platform scaffolds...sidewalk sheds that protected the public by covering the sidewalks were a form of platform scaffold, and had to be inspected every day.

Whenever possible, we tried to use something other than a scaffold to reach the work. Articulated manlifts saved a project from using exterior scaffolding on a school construction job in Queens once. I was relieved, as this particular contractor had been terrible about maintaining scaffolds on other jobs.

One weekend job in particular had a really large, building-enfolding scaffold: the former NYC Board of Education headquarters at 110 Livingston Street in Brooklyn. I spent half the day checking it, but then the only work that weekend on the 12-story building was off the scaffold or on the roof. The really fun part about that job was that you had to get on and off of the scaffold by entering a window and carefully walking through the offices of touchy bureaucrats. They were much more concerned about you scratching their mahogany desk than a worker falling off the scaffold to his or her death.

For what it's worth, I did have a man on one of my sites fall off a scaffold once. His was a short fall, all of four feet onto a soft pile of sand. He split his pants. Duct tape fixed that enough to maintain decency.

It was always nice when a potentially lethal incident could be fixed with duct tape.

NYU, and Winter Mud

By winter, the Union Street apartment house project in Brooklyn was turned over to someone else and I was transferred to a project in Manhattan.

New York University Hospital at 34th Street on 2nd Avenue wanted to add a research facility. It was in back of their main building, along the FDR Drive. Part of the new facility was going to be built on an existing building that had been demolished to ground level; they were gutting the basement, which was open on one side, like a cave. The rest of the job was, at this point, foundation work for a new structure next to that. This new building was not going to be on solid rock. Sightseeing tip: you can scan the Manhattan skyline and instantly see what's built on solid rock, since that's where all the really tall buildings are. So the first step for this new foundation was to drill shafts down into the bedrock, and fill them with concrete so the building would be firmly attached to that deep anchor.

The only problem was that it was bitterly cold out, and that cold was made worse by an arctic wind that swept down along the rivers from the north. All of the work at this point was outside in that icy environment.

Now I love working out of doors, but there are limits to what I can tolerate. Even though I wore at least five layers of clothing I was pretty darned frozen unless I kept moving. I wore two pairs of long thermal underwear, jeans, and sweatpants over those on my lower half. My torso had two pairs of thermals, a long-sleeved cotton shirt, a sweater, and a sweatshirt. Then there was a Carhart one-piece thermal construction cold suit that went over it all. For my head, I had two polar fleece headscarves that went under my hard hat with a wool scarf over those that I breathed in through. You had to breathe *out* through your mouth or you'd fog up your safety glasses. Oh, and the safety glasses which were usually too hot were not just for eye hazards: they kept your eyeballs a little warmer. On my feet were two pairs of socks: cotton inside, wool outside, with a plastic bag in between - all stuffed inside oversized waterproofed and insulated boots. My hands were covered in layers, too: cotton gloves, plastic gloves, wool gloves, and mittens - and then shoved in my pockets.

Confessions of a Female Safety Engineer

I looked like a Michelin Man on his way to Antarctica. And I put most of it on before I left for work, driving with the car's heat off and the windows cracked open so I would not overheat.

Trying to take off even some of that to use the rest room, which was in the superintendent's trailer, was pretty epic. And whenever I did that, the superintendent would growl at me that *"The job's outside!"* Admittedly, he was out there most of the time but he made it clear that my even using the rest room should be kept short. I was to help him reach zero injuries on this job, which was fine with me, but the man was abrasive. I consoled myself that when the regular safety manager who was on this site was recovered from his car accident, he could *have* this place.

I managed, until one day I walked into the equivalent of frozen quicksand. You see, the temperatures were way below freezing. So when they drilled those shafts toward the bedrock, they mixed the water that brought up the mud slurry with antifreeze. I walked up onto what I thought was a hill of frozen dirt. But it was a hill of muddy antifreeze slurry and I sank down into it, up to my hips. Thank God there were workers nearby. It took two strong men to haul me out. I was wet from the waist down, and in danger of frostbite.

The kindly workers set me up near a propane heater in a private "room" which was really a cargo box with a door. You've seen such rectangular metal boxes, like on a cargo ship or the back of a semi or as a railroad car. These cargo boxes are very often used as a construction shanties—a place to change clothes and store tools—on outdoor jobs. I stayed in there, warming up and drying off, until it was time to go home.

The wonderful workers covered my absence with the nasty superintendent for me. And luckily I had a tarp in my car to sit on while driving on the way home. I always tried to keep a change of clothing with me after that.

There was one other job that involved a real mess. But that was another transit job. And this time it was not mud, it was sand. *Lots* of sand.

Jamaica Yard

THE NY TRANSIT TRAIN MAINTENANCE YARD IN JAMAICA, QUEENS WAS JUST south of Flushing Bay, and Flushing Meadow Park—home of the Unisphere and US Open Tennis—and was built on a swamp. This was good in that I was a birder, and I enjoyed seeing all the colorful songbirds in spring migration. This was bad, in that water got into everything.

The contractor was mainly removing old hydrants and adding new ones along a road that had sunk twice in the last 50 years. All of his excavations for new hydrant pipes had to be constantly pumped dry so they could work in them, and all of them required trench shields to keep the muddy soil from overwhelming the men in the shallow trenches. There was a train repair shed—really a big long barn that barn swallows lived in—and a train wash, rather like a drive-through carwash with tracks. North of the train shed was a little drier, and that's where we kept the heavy equipment and put the construction trailers, with sandpipers running all over the little sand dunes behind our office.

This was the site where I played doorman to patient barn swallows swirling above each side of the exterior doors, waiting for a human to let them through. This was the site where I tried to straddle a skinny excavation with my car and misjudged where my wheels were, and my car had to be hauled out with slings. And this was the site where I basically got buried in sand.

Whenever we had to go across a road with an excavation, it was a disruption to 24-hour, seven-days-a-week train yard operations until the road was reopened. So if the work took more than one day, when we left we covered that open trench in the roadway with a huge steel plate so that traffic could get through until we came back.

One beautiful spring day, while I was doing some paperwork in my car with my window open, our excavator rumbled past. The heavy equipment operator was moving one of those steel plates, which was clutched in the excavator bucket's jaws. (Clutched in its jaws was good; I'd seen a heavy equipment operator almost decapitated by a steel plate he merely balanced on his bucket.)

93

Confessions of a Female Safety Engineer

As the excavator rumbled past my open car window, it hit a bump. And all of the dried sandy soil that had been stuck to the huge steel plate came loose and slid down into my car, mainly through my open car window and into my lap. Eight inches of sand! I got out, sputtering, and shook myself off. The men laughed and laughed. So did I. It was pretty funny.

After we got the worst of the sandy mess out of my car with a shovel, I drove my poor vehicle to a local car wash. The guys at the vacuum station looked absolutely horrified when they saw the sandbox that had been my car's interior. I tipped them heavily for helping me. They deserved every penny.

Jamaica Yard had one other funny thing happen. Out in the main yard, where the train interiors were being scrubbed and the train cars' burned-out light bulbs changed, there were huge light stands for night work. You've probably seen the same sort of tall ring lights at major cloverleaf intersections on the interstate, but these also had loudspeakers on them, so that the yard management could make announcements.

One day I was inspecting our trenches and heard a deafening noise behind me. "What the heck was that?" I asked a passing NYC Transit worker.

He pointed to a nearby light stand, grinning.

I saw nothing.

"It's a bird," he explained.

I looked up again and saw a tiny bird on the light stand, and frowned. "That little thing?"

He laughed as he explained that some of the birds had figured out how to use the hollow loudspeakers as electrified megaphones. That was what I was hearing, a Godzilla-sized *TWEEEET*!

Hilarious.

⚠

Of course it was not all fun and games. There was an enormous amount of paperwork. I had to prepare and deliver a safety briefing every day, do safety preplanning, and deal with about ten kinds of inspectors.

About this time Transit decided to put their train track flaggers under the Site Safety Manager's control, and I had to watch them like a hawk. Some of them were quite professional but not all. I had never seen such incredibly lazy, rebellious, stupid people as the bottom of that particular barrel. They'd sit on the wooden cover for a live third rail if you did not stop them.

Once, they showed up for a Saturday GO in the yard that was slated to run for 14 hours during late Autumn. It got dark early but they had not brought their signal lanterns. So at dusk they were just going to leave us with our work unfinished and go home. They said were going to report us to their bosses for trying to make them work without signal lights.

I was furious. I quoted their own regulations to their foreman, and asked *them* if they'd like me to report them to their transit inspector, since they had not brought their absolutely required signal lanterns, required even for a job that would not happen in the dark. The contractor and I scrounged up enough flashlights from our cars for them to use as signal lanterns and they stayed, sullen and resentful, bunched up in one area. A quick, surreptitious call had Transit's safety inspector catching them not spread out like they were supposed to be, to cover the blind curves.

I made the dreaded inspectors my allies on many a job with a recalcitrant contractor, too. Building Department, insurance inspector, transit safety...once I was sure they'd work with me I'd call them and ask for their help getting a devious or reluctant crew to follow rules. Like a safety manager, safety inspectors for the government or insurance companies knew that these rules that had been written in someone's blood, written when someone else had gotten hurt. These inspectors had the same goal as I did—a safe, injury-free job—and they were *less* likely to write us up if I asked for their help. We were on the same side, fighting for the same thing. I felt they were my friends and teammates.

Of course, to the contractor who wanted to close a street without DOT permits or work with inadequate fall protection, the inspectors *just happened* to show up at the worst possible time and shut them down. I was the unsafe contractor's sympathetic friend, the genius that talked the nasty inspector out of writing them up. And oh, by the way, here was an easy way to follow the rules and keep that bastard inspector off your back next time.

You've no idea how heretical my attitude was. After all, everyone knew the inspectors were our enemies! Really? Not most of them. We all wanted a safe job, I thought, so why not work together?

Confessions of a Female Safety Engineer

Some of the inspectors that had no rules against it so once I even an arrangements where an insurance inspector and I would let our bosses expense our lunch together, his boss this month, my boss next month. After all, a good relationship between us was great for the job.

I did whatever it took made the job safe, so that "my" men went home in one piece. And despite some their best efforts to kill themselves they did go home safely. My buddies the safety inspectors and I made sure of that.

The Fatal Few

OFTEN THE FOCUS OF THESE SAFETY INSPECTORS WERE DICTATED BY RECENT, highly-publicized incidents. They'd react with what were called "safety stand downs," which would be throughout a whole company, or a whole government agency. So a fire would prompt the city agencies to make you retrain and look at fire protection. A crane collapse would have them scrutinize all cranes in the City and you'd have to retrain your crew on the new guidelines. Things falling off of buildings would have them inspecting with a view to avoid such falling objects in the future, and you'd have to be diligent and get your men to be, too.

In between these externally imposed emergencies, I got to choose what potential hazard to train the men about, and the focus of my inspections to reduce that particular site's current dangers.

We safety managers all swore allegiance to the concept of "zero injuries," but really, all we as risk managers could do was aim for that. If the City or OSHA were not pushing a particular safety issue, I tried to look at injury management via something called the Pareto Principle. Vilfredo Pareto (1848-1923) was the man who first realized that 20 percent of almost any system is responsible for 80 percent of the results.

For me as a safety engineer, it meant that 20 percent of all injuries were responsible for 80 percent *of the costs*. Now that I was working on "major buildings"—large projects—the people I worked for were not just looking for "lower insurance rates." My clients were mostly self-insured. So it was important stop onsite injuries and illnesses, but it was especially important to cut down on the expensive ones. These injuries and illnesses tend to be personally expensive to the person who is harmed, so I had a deeper reason to halt such injuries. At the head of the list of expensive injuries were back strains. I did a lot of "how to lift correctly" training. I even brought in a chiropractor to teach a crew not to twist while lifting ; your body's not built to do that.

Early in my career, one appliance warehouse client I consulted for had such a problem. They had a delivery crew, and their delivery people were having a huge number of back injuries, despite how-to-lift training. So I was asked to ride along with them for a day and see why they were having so many incidents. Short version: they were paid by the piece, by the delivery, and not by the hour. They had an economic incentive to not only rush when lugging a refrigerator up the stairs, but to speed in their truck. My recommendations were to pay them by the hour, give them a 10-minute group stretch in the mornings, and put a "How's my driving?" sticker with a toll-free number on each truck.

But that was not a construction safety environment.

By the time I was in construction safety I was heartily jealous of my fellow safety managers that worked in industrial safety, like in that warehouse. Safety managers working at established industrial clients had an injury history and could look at site injury trends. They had the luxury of equipment that was bolted to the floor, walls that did not move, and stable personnel.

Construction sites, especially new ones, have no injury history look for trends. Walls went up overnight, changing the routes to fire exits. Equipment was moved, sometimes daily, sometimes hourly. Despite safety orientations any workers that came in were not really screened. In comparison to industrial safety, construction safety was an absolute madhouse. And all could I base recommendations on was trends in the typical injury history of each trade. My best source for that was the Bureau of Labor Statistics.

Such analyses led to strange places, at times. For example, construction workers in general are more likely to injure themselves on a Monday or a Friday, when their minds were not entirely on their work, and they are especially at risk the day before a major holiday. Some of that risk was alcohol related, as in coming in with a hangover or taking a nip on the job. You learned when to watch for such things.

Construction workers, like industrial workers, were more likely to get hurt doing non-routine tasks. This was why such things as bringing a crane on site were safety preplanned so the dangerous non-routine tasks were at least thought through in advance.

So, since 20 percent of all hazards on my construction sites would account for 80 percent of all the men's injuries, I tried to target that 20%.

Within that 20 percent I was especially careful to avoid situations that led to deaths: there was a selection of hazards we call The Fatal Few. These were, according to the most recent stats (2014):

- Falls - 359 out of 899 total deaths in construction in were falls (39.9%)
- Electrocutions - 74 deaths were from electricity (8.2%)
- Struck by Object - 73 deaths were from being hit by something (not a vehicle) (8.1%)
- Caught-in/between - 39 of the deaths were...squish* (4.3%)
  *This category includes construction workers killed when caught-in or compressed by equipment or objects, and struck, caught, or crushed in collapsing structure, equipment, or material.

Obviously, falls were THE fatality risk in construction, the main killer. And certain trades were more exposed to falls. Ironworkers, especially, took huge risks when erecting steel and there were all sorts of strategies to keep them safe. You could weld on the guardrails and add steel cables to the beams on the ground, *before* they were lifted by crane and bolted to the edges of a new floor. Or you could outfit your steel erectors with 150-ft retractable steel safety lanyards that would stop a fall while they erected steel or made things safe. Past a certain height NYC code required debris netting, which might also catch a falling human.

But everyone was at risk if the guardrails were left open at an elevator shaft, or the edge protection railings of a building were broken or defective. I worked on very some tall buildings, and the price of safety was eternal vigilance.

Guts, as I noted earlier, are pink. I did not want evidence of that on any of my sites.

The Green Building,
Battery Park City

Construction in lower Manhattan slowly resumed about a year after 9/11.

One of the jobs to restart once the rubble of the twin towers was mostly cleared was something we called The Green Building. It was in Battery Park City, an area of Manhattan owned not by NYC, but by the State of New York. It was a bit of real estate where NY State conducted experiments and showcased things like new infrastructure design and innovative building design.

For this project, they were building a very energy-efficient residential high rise that made some of its own power, was set up for storing bicycles, and was constructed with low VOC or natural materials: things like wool carpets, no-formaldehyde insulation batting, and paint with low fumes. The decorative trim lines gracing the sides of the building were made out of solar panels, and each roof either had gardens or they were green roofs covered with soil and low, spreading vegetation that reflected less heat into an urban environment.

It was also one of the more fascinating neighborhoods I had ever been posted in. NYPD mounted police shared the location with us, and I got into the habit of bringing in carrots and apples for the horses. The site was across a slim street from the southern tip of the very long and narrow Hudson River Park. The main buildings that housed the Tribeca Film Festival were to our south (working during the film festival was nuts: no parking, nowhere with a table free to eat lunch....)

I spent many a lunch break seated near a koi pond in Hudson River Park as it continued on its way a block south to the World Financial Center. And then there a monument to the Irish potato famine, a cottage and landscape disassembled in Ireland and reassembled here.

The World Financial Center itself had numerous only-slightly-overpriced places to eat. Its famous Winter Garden was inside, which I was disappointed to discover was nothing more than a bunch of tall, lonely palm trees in a big greenhouse, surrounded by sterile tile steps. But there was a river-view outdoor restaurant in the back, surrounded with low concrete waterfalls, where our client threw a couple of parties I was invited to. Nice.

The parties came later. When I got there, due to tensions on this site, the consulting company I worked for was about to lose this client: one of our largest customers. The client's new corporate safety inspector, Pete, was a man who used to be an OSHA inspector, and in the military before that. He simply could not get it through his head that he could not do safety by decree. Yes, we all wanted to follow the rules, but it was his way or the highway.

Yet, we liked the guy. So my fellow safety engineers and I all conspired to bring him gently into the civilian world.

The reason the previous safety manager had been rotated out was that he and Pete had a disagreement about how to implement a confined space entry. A confined space is something that has only one way to get in or out, and is not meant for continuous human habitation: something like a fuel tank. It could also be a pit at least 5 feet deep where you might have trapped gasses that were heavier than air. And there are two kinds of confined spaces. The more dangerous kind of confined space is permit-only entry, which requires continuous air monitoring, a full time monitor worker and emergency extraction gear (like in those river-water cooling pipes at the World Trade Center). A non-permit required confined space is one where you test the air in it, and the atmosphere is fine.

The client's former OSHA safety guy Pete insisted that something on the site was a permit-required confined space, but the contractor's superintendent and my fellow safety engineer disagreed with him. So they ran a non-permit confined space entry over the weekend without telling Pete, and when he found out, Pete hit the roof.

Now, personally, I agreed with my fellow safety manager: it was a place where if you did the air monitoring and it checked out fine, there was no reason to worry. But their way of implementing it was ham-fisted, and direct insubordination to the company we had a contract with that paid us. Not smart.

I solved the trust breach with the help of another safety manager who was back to work at the cold, muddy site I'd covered during his recovery from a car accident. We were so excited about implementing this fix that we had a loud, enthusiastic strategy session on the Long Island Rail Road early one morning when the other commuters were trying to sleep and giving us the stink eye. We had not realized we'd gotten loud and tried to tone it down. But we were on a roll.

The current contentious safety issue had to do with Fall Protection. All of the rooms that were adjacent to the 18-story hoist we had just taken down were open to the elements and presented a serious fall hazard. Anyone could walk in there! And there were no anchor points to tie the men off to put in railings. Pete the corporate safety guy wanted all sorts of elaborate fall protection gear worn by anyone in those rooms, and signage, and all sorts of training. Instead, we engineered out the hazard and got Pete to sign off on it, in advance.

First, our new plan was to put keyed locks on each room from the hall, keys that only the superintendents had, so they knew when someone was in there. Presto: not just 'anyone' could wander in. Next, we proposed one trained crew should add NYC code safety railings to openings on each floor; these wire rope barricades are higher than OSHA railings with an extra midrail, and have orange ¼-inch debris netting. The men putting those up wore fall protection gear tied to a horizontal life line. That lifeline stretched down the hall to anchor points where they were anchored to short sections of brick and steel wall in between two windows at each end.

Pete signed off on the plan, and everyone loved it except the superintendent, who was angry that he was left holding the keys, and wanted to grind Pete's nose into the dust after how much trouble he'd gotten into over the confined space.

Site management was happy with me, except the superintendent who had been reined in. I ignored him. Later, he got his revenge by keeping me off a site he was running so he was free to do things his way. He got someone killed and lost his job. Oops.

⚠

I should mention that this was a site where I was the only female on staff. Even the admin was male, at least at first. So The Green Building site was where I started wearing my hard hat in the office, without fail, because if I didn't United Parcel Service, the postman, and FedEx would all walk past the male admin to my desk in the back, to get me to sign for packages. I was the only female in the room, so I must be the flunky, eh? When they saw the hard hat you could see their unconscious assumptions grind to a halt, though. They'd stop, looking confused. *Wait a minute, secretaries don't wear hard hats.* Once in a while they would even find the male admin without any assistance from me at all.

What you wore was important in a lot of ways. Team wear for the companies involved, not sportswear, was the ultimate safety incentive prize. Men would compete for it. The guys in the field might mock me, and leave less-than-flattering sketches and graffiti around the site to taunt me, but they still wanted the fancy new jacket with my company's logo I'd gotten as a thank you. Bling and clothes that had the contractor, union, or supplier's name on them carried cachet according to an unwritten rule: the more expensive the item, the more street cred and better bragging rights you got. The ultimate coup was to have a quilted baseball jacket or a leather jacket with the company or supplier or union logo. So jackets from a recognizable gift source were hot and implied you were somebody.

After the danger of our losing this client was all over, I came back to my desk in the client's construction trailer complex, wearing my much-coveted new company logo jacket. I found the boss of Consulting Inc. waiting for me with his feet up at my desk, wearing *his* fancy new company logo jacket, too.

"Nice jacket," I commented dryly, walking past him to set down my things, not bowing and scraping but using ironic humor which he totally got.

He just wanted to make sure I understood he appreciated me saving the client for him. I was going to be employee of the month (again.) That came with a $100 bonus.

How nice, I thought to myself, *considering how little you pay me.* But I smiled and thanked him. And I kept my hard hat on.

In Praise of Turtles

HARD HATS ARE AMAZING.

They are built to be able to stand an eight-pound weight dropped from five feet up, and the kinds worn in construction need to be able to protect you from electrical shock. The shock-suspension webbing inside them also protects a worker from the force of an impact hurting their neck and spine.

One job I was on had a man who'd had his life saved by a hard hat when the sling lifting some structural steel off a truck he was next to gave way, and a piece of steel actually glanced off his head. It was a good-sized piece of steel, too.

There is an award I was able to give out for when a hard hat saves someone's life, where the person it saves becomes a member of the Turtle Club. Here's the story of a man on one of my sites who got a Turtle certificate. He was wearing his hard hat in a place you'd not think you needed one, and it protected him from a very unexpected hazard.

We were working on a building that had its structural steel erected, but was not entirely encased in the brick and window walls that would enclose it. The emergency fire stair the man walked up was still open above, because they were going to add a smoke hatch on top. They were still using a crane to bring up bundles of Q-decking to a floor above the stair. The stacks of Q-deck (wavy stainless steel base for poured concrete floors) were held together with steel band strapping, with two-by-fours on the corners to keep the decking from cutting the band strapping.

One of the bands broke anyhow, and the two-by-four underneath it flipped into the air, then plummeted down the open stairwell and hit this fellow on his hard hat eight floors down. Without his head protection, he'd be messily dead.

Yet I had serious problems getting some of the men to wear their hard hats. Yes, they're hot in the summer but they also provide shade and you can wear a wet bandana underneath. And, no, it's not okay to take a drill and air condition your hard hat full of holes.

Confessions of a Female Safety Engineer

Hard hats were also where we safety managers put orientation stickers. To a large extent, the color of a hard hat told you what trade a man was in: blue for electricians, a brown netting design for steel erectors, yellow meant laborer, green meant plumber, and white was management.

The one gold hard hat I saw on a rather vain project manager and the bright pink one saw a female insurance auditor wearing just meant that they were weird.

On Roosevelt Island

AFTER A BRIEF STINT ON AN **OSHA** VOLUNTARY PROTECTION PROGRAM (VPP) in Queens I was sent to a hospital project and adjacent ball field some contractor client was building on Roosevelt Island.

An OSHA VPP site is a partnership with OSHA where the client would not be written up and OSHA was their *partner* in making the site as safe as possible. This VPP project was to be the site of a new mall on a formerly contaminated site in Queens. The part of that job I was involved in was the prefab concrete construction of a parking garage, with all sorts of leading edge fall protection nightmares, and it was great practice in writing up things to show OSHA where I had engineered something that was as safe or safer than their regulation routines, in a situation where those regulation routines were impractical.

I had worked on industrial safety with something similar at Ciba-Geigy, which was an OSHA Star Program site, the highest level of OSHA VPP. The difference was that this VPP site is a construction site and mostly under OHSA's construction standards (CFR 1926), while the OSHA Star program at Ciba-Geigy was industrial and mostly under their general industry standards (CFR 1910). For my part, I needed to know both sets of OSHA standards, because there was a lot of overlap. OSHA's construction standards, especially, referenced their general industry standards. And both referenced other standards such as ANSI (the American National Standards Institute, which regulates materials science), NFPA (the National Fire Protection Association), or the NEC (National Electric Code). I was building up quite a library of reference books!

But then my employer whisked me off to an island.

Where and what is Roosevelt Island, you say? For those of you who have never been to New York City, perhaps you remember a fight scene in the first *Spiderman* movie, the dramatic battle over the East River involving suspended cable cars. That's the tramway between downtown and Roosevelt Island. The dead mansion at Roosevelt Island's southern tip of is also where they filmed the final fight between Spiderman and the Green Goblin. Usually, NYC sets off most of its big Fourth of July Fireworks from that same ruined mansion.

So there I was, on that long sliver of land in the middle of the East River. And I mean long: Roosevelt Island parallels Manhattan from 45th Street to 84th Street. It's technically within the borough of Manhattan, but all the real estate on it belongs to the State of New York, just like Battery Park City. The island is a quiet little residential enclave in the noisy city, full of parks and ball fields. It's not all that easy to get to, and has its own little shops and cultural things. It's a world unto itself. And any industry on Roosevelt Island is quiet. It's mostly specialty hospitals. Several of them even have that view of three red and white smokestacks made famous in the movie *Conspiracy Theory*.

My client was building another specialty hospital just north of where the Queensboro Bridge passes overhead, bisecting the sliver of an island. The weather was lovely, it was spring, and I enjoyed the warming sun outside when I was not tearing my hair out at the ridiculous lack of safety on this particular site, at least until I brought it up to speed.

I was getting quite a reputation within my company for straightening out difficult sites. The first day I was at this one, I wrote what was probably my favorite thing I ever put into a Site Safety Manager's daily log: "Beer cans shall not be used as rebar caps."

I'd been on sites with drinking problems before, like the one where the superintendent did not think he had a problem so I carefully picked up a full black trash bag of beer cans from his site parking lot and plunked them down on his desk.

He looked inside the bag, and paled, shutting it quickly. "Has anyone else seen these?" he asked me, alarmed.

"No," I assured him.

"I'll take care of it," he promised, dragging the full trash bag with him, and he did.

But here, at this site on Roosevelt Island, the beer cans were not just all over the parking area. They were stuck on pikes like heads, covering a row of metal rebar rods sticking up right by the main entrance, all of the cans proudly on display.

My camera was my friend. I took the cans down because you did not want that tableau setting the mood for an inspector, but not before I took a photo to share with my new client's superintendent.

He looked at the display on my camera and paled. "Has anyone else seen this?" he asked me.

"No," I assured him.

"I'll take care of it," he promised. And he did.

"Can you erase that photo?" he also asked. And I did. But not before I was sure I wouldn't need it to push him again.

Actual orange rebar caps to protect the men from impalement hazards went on those pieced of rebar. We got that site ship shape, in a hurry.

⚠

Speaking of ships, the little bridge to Roosevelt Island from Queens (there is no bridge to Manhattan) could not handle the huge crane we brought in to put HVAC units on the roof of the new hospital. So we brought the crane in via river barge. That was fine, except this crane was so heavy it would tear up the roads getting the rest of the way to our site. So we came up with an innovative solution. Plywood sheets were put in front of the treads as it came off the barge and laid in front of it as it crawled along. We used the tops of the continuous tracks (the larger cranes all have treads like tanks) as sort of a conveyer belt to bring sheets of plywood up front as it drove forward, then we put each sheet down in front of it again. Plywood leapfrog! It took several laborers moving these sheet over an hour to get the crane from the barge to our site, but that was still much cheaper than resurfacing a road.

I would have loved to stay on this project. But I was only there for another safety manager's vacation relief. By April I was assigned elsewhere, to a more long-term job.

Essex and Delancey

UNDERNEATH DELANCEY STREET, JUST OFF THE MANHATTAN SIDE OF THE Williamsburg Bridge, is a complex of interconnected subway stations called Essex and Delancey. Here trains that use the bridge instead of dipping underneath the East River finally dive underground to join the warren of subway tunnels under Manhattan. Just underground, before the station, is the site of a huge abandoned horse-drawn cable car turnaround, complete with ancient cable car tracks.

Our underground construction trailers were on the edge of the old cable car turnaround. Such a large space that was barely used intrigued me. I soon learned there was good reason to leave it be.

This time the Local 3 electricians were on the right side of a dispute. Their shop steward, whose position was traditionally the point man for safety issues, came to me one day. He made sure no one saw him enter or leave my office. He feared for his job if seen talking to me, and he also feared for his men. He told me that most of the turnaround was enclosed in a fence that was marked "Danger, Lead." The lead dated back to when the cable cars were in used in the 1800s, never mind how. And my new general contractor client, who had not covered themselves with safety glory by getting some poor man's legs crushed by a heavy wire cable spool careening down the public subway stairs before my arrival, was storing materials *inside that fence*.

A snap decision was thrust on me. I could not write up my own client. And although because I worked for a consulting firm so that I *could* leave if a client would not behave, *should* I walk away unless I solved this mess? No. The men down here were at risk.

If there was one theme to my safety work, it was me being a fierce mama bear protecting her cubs. I was assigned here. These were "my" men. I'd fight for them. But I'd have to be subtle.

I assured the shop steward I'd go to bat before him behind the scenes. For now, he should know that while that lead contamination was dangerous, it

111

was fairly easy to prevent getting contaminated. For now, until I solved this, I showed him how to protect his men. He would be responsible for disseminating this information through the trades on site, through the other shop stewards.

Lead is heavy, and it tends to settle on surfaces and on the floor. The primary route for contamination is ingestion, so he should instruct his men to use very careful hygiene and wash their hands before eating, smoking, or drinking. The men should remove their shoes when they left the site and change their clothes as soon as they got home before they hugged or touched anyone, washing the possibly contaminated clothes separately. This was especially important if there were children in the house.

And, I joked to ease the tension, whatever you do, don't lick the floor out there.

I gave him some untraceable literature on lead safety, and he snuck out with it. After I checked out the site to see if what the shop steward said was true, I would run the situation past my employers and let my boss threaten this GC behind closed doors. It was always preferable to bring a contractor around to a safe way of thinking than it was to get them arrested, but what were my options? My boss would not want me to lose a client, but he did not want to sued as part of the problem, either. And we might be sued unless I moved fast. What were the *men's options*, lose their job or get ill? I'd just met a tile man, an older artisan who married late in life and had a new baby daughter at home who was the light of his life; any lead contamination he brought home could harm his child. I could *not* abandon these people.

Dear God, what a mess.

I went out to do some discrete reconnaissance. Yes, the fence was open and the lead warning signs were there posted on it, albeit darkened with a century of the usual steel and concrete dust that covers the subways, but legible if you looked. And there was a shortcut with recent traffic that cut through the lead area enclosure—from the trailers to the work—with a string of inadequate construction lights above it. A pile of new lumber and cases of tile had been placed near the walkway inside the enclosure. Totally unacceptable.

I went up to the street level to find an out-of-the-way place to call my boss and fill him in. He came by later, to look, so that it was his observations he complained about and not a case of me reporting them. That was useful: they'd resent me if I stayed and they thought I was a "snitch."

What trickled back to me of my boss's conversation with the unsafe general contractor client was a litany of excuses on their part, and the distant noise of a hammer coming down. Were they out of their minds? If NYC transit's environmental department found out about this, this contractor would never work for transit again. It sounded like my boss basically threatened, with no witnesses, to untraceably leak what they were doing to the authorities *and the press*. He also threatened to pull any safety managers from this site unless they behaved. He was in a position of power since there were not enough safety managers and Transit needed track-trained safety managers far more than they needed another contractor. Why couldn't they do the right thing and store their materials somewhere else?

The contractor caved. Soon, the materials were no longer stored in the lead enclosure, and the gates to it were padlocked shut; the shortcut through the hazardous area was abandoned. Transit's environmental department came through and did testing, and slated the area for a cleanup. New signs were put up, warning everyone to keep out until they had abated the hazard.

The tile man with the new baby daughter, as well as all of the rest of the men on the site, were now safe. And later on they must had done the lead abatement, since the area is now slated to become an underground park: The Lowline.

⚠️

As I said, this was a long-term assignment. The Essex & Delancey job neighborhood was within walking distance of the famed Katz's Deli and I was able to visit it, once. But there were great things closer. Almost every day I visited the Essex Street Market, an indoor farmers' market and fresh market for things like breads and cheeses. The Essex market booths were inexpensive and it brought needed healthy food to the neighborhood at a reasonable price. I'd buy mangoes, or watermelon, or flowers , or fresh fruit there every day.

The topside market was a nice break from my subterranean existence at this job. We were fully renovating two stations—mostly the station for the J and M lines, with a side order of the station for the Z and the F lines—and these were connected with a warren of underground passages where I was in serious danger of running into homeless "residents." Transit laid poison baits down there for the rats, too. In honor of that my men cheerfully tried to bait me with a rubber rat that "breathed" when they pumped a bladder through a hose; but it was so fake looking that I just rolled my eyes.

The official entrance to the construction trailers and work areas was a temporarily closed subway entrance, but we could get in out at no less than eight other subway entrances and exits for the J, M Z and F trains.

Above the subway stations were a series of air vents. You've probably seen the iconic photo of Marylin Monroe with her skirt puffed up by a sidewalk vent underneath her? That was the sort of vent we were repairing and replacing. That meant closing sidewalks to break up the concrete and re-pour them. And that sort of work required permits from the DOT.

The Department Of Transportation took the position that they owned the sidewalks of NYC. That was a not an unreasonable concept since so much foot traffic went over them and if you closed a sidewalk the foot traffic might end up in a busy street. But, more importantly, there were sometimes things under those sidewalks: buried communications or electrical wires, or vent shafts that fed air to the subway tunnels.

There were no other utilities underneath the sidewalks we had to disrupt, except subway air vents. But there were so many sidewalks that needed redone that, despite being an NYC Transit job, we attracted City inspectors to see if we were following our DOT permits.

Ah, the DOT permits. There were, between lane closures, sidewalk closures, or permissions to park dumpsters or heavy equipment on the street, forty-eight DOT permits for this job. It was very confusing, so I tried to make them easier to work with. I sorted the permits based on what street they pertained to, and hand-numbered the permits. Then made a map of the streets involved, and put the numbers of the permits on the map as a key. If nothing else, my homemade DOT permit map got the safety inspectors out of my hair in record time.

This job did not have any BEST Squad inspectors from the Department of Buildings downstairs. But it had lots of NYC transit safety inspectors to make up for it. They came to oversee particularly touchy work like our using a subway entry stair to bring down supplies: they had a real concern after that leg-crushing incident. We closed the stairs when we had to make any deliveries that might injure, and all cable spools had guide ropes that created a failsafe if the men carrying the spools lost their grip on the things.

I suppose you've noticed that some subway lines have numerical designators (like 1, 3, or 7) and other have letters like J, M or F. There is an interesting reason for that, and it has to do with the history of New York City.

The early train lines in New York were all private lines, run as businesses. They were eventually all bought up by the City and made into a coherent system, but the numerical lines have a wider tunnels than the alphabet lines. The numerical lines, by and large, seem to go north/south through Manhattan and up into the Bronx, with the notable exception of the #7 line that goes over to Queens, and spurs at the bottom of the 2, 3, 4, and 5 lines that cross into Brooklyn.

My overtime during this period was on the # 7 Line, night work where the men were stripping lead paint and repainting columns, and finishing installing tile on the walls. It was down below the NY Public Library, but might as well have been on the moon since that neighborhood was dead at night.

Alphabet Streets, and Con Ed

My next posting had me exploring a part of NYC I'd never seen before. Avenues A through D bump out to the east of 1st Avenue in lower Manhattan, between Stuyvesant Town and Houston. The western part of the Alphabet district is culturally part of the *avant-garde* East Village. The neighborhood gets pretty nondescript when you head east toward the FDR Drive.

And on the edge of the edge of the FDR drive is the largest Con Ed Power plant in New York City. It's placed there because of the deep harbor; it's tank can suck up entire supertankers full of oil to run its massive boilers.

There was no easy way to get to this part of the city via mass transit, so I had to drive. I and the men I worked with paid for our parking on the massive sidewalk in front of the plant with occasional, and expected, parking tickets. Many of us kept that cost down by carpooling and splitting the ticket fees. It was just the cost of doing business.

Everything inside this power plant was enormous: the boilers, the pipes, the wiring, the potential problems. And the control room was like something right out of NASA.

The firm that contracted for my services as a consulting engineer had a contract to do some demolition in this cavernous facility, and the project manager was none other than Sam, the guy who'd been my project manager on my first safety job all those years ago. It was like old home week. It was so good to see him. I met his crew and got a briefing on the work. Demolition always worried me, but everything would be fine as long as they carefully followed my directions.

Con Ed put us all through a severe safety briefing, with an emphasis on not getting complacent and blasé around high voltage lines and equipment. Their brief training film, "I Got Comfortable" was narrated by a man who'd lost both his arms in a high voltage explosion. It was sobering. Then we learned the little nuances of their safety routines, like ALWAYS having earplugs with you, visible, no matter what.

117

Confessions of a Female Safety Engineer

We also learned about the young mother who'd recently died of heat stress when another contractor had been removing boiler asbestos a couple of months back.

Although her death was due to heat stress, I shuddered for another reason. Boilers like that typically have a serious asbestos problem, especially older ones. Asbestos, as a mineral, has several forms and one of the most dangerous of them all—crocidolite, blue asbestos—is what goes around things like boilers.

We were going to be doing demolition in a building crawling with all sorts of asbestos hazards.

Let me tell you about the asbestos removal project that went wrong.

Remember when I said that if they followed my directions, things would be fine? Short version: they didn't listen. They'd done just fine cleaning out certain rooms of asbestos and demolishing the walls. But I had shown them what block asbestos insulation looked like and where it was.

All I had to do was go on a bathroom break. And before I went back into the building I got a call that the crew had done unprotected demolition on a block asbestos wall I'd *warned* them about, and we were all thrown off the job.

During this project period there was a woman who would be a part of the later attempted unionization of our "trade." We'll call her Michelle. She worked for a major subcontractor on this failed demolition and abatement project, as the site admin, but she was into everything. In retrospect everything she did on that Con Ed site was to one end: to gather information so that she could be a power in a new union composed of nothing but licensed NYC Site Safety Managers.

THE TALE OF THE
LABORIOUS LABOR LEECHES

MY IMMEDIATE SUPERVISOR, JOHN, WAS A PAIN TO WORK WITH. BUT THE company's other supervisor, Terry, was much easier to get along with. He also had a slightly different background: John used to be an NYC building inspector, while Terry used to be with the FDNY. So if I had a fire-related question, I would often call Terry for advice. He was always nice to talk to, and he told really great instructive stories.

But Terry would always warn me not to tell John I'd called him about anything, because John was short-tempered and touchy about such things. That fit with my experiences with John, too, so I kept our conversations secret. Little did I know that Terry had a more important reason for keeping our chats private. He had been carefully working for two years to change our field forever, and not in a good way.

Terry, Michelle from that sub at Con Ed, and one other person all wanted to turn Licensed NYC Site Safety managers into a unionized trade. They were gonna be the union bigwigs, making a killing off our dues. And for what?

The proposed union rules were insidious, trying to force the same standards as other unions to our "trade" and they simply did not fit. Whereas designations apprentice, journeyman, and master worked for things like plumbers and electricians, and could have logical pay jumps as you went up a grade, I felt they simply did not apply to what safety managers did.

First of all, we were management. You don't, as a rule, unionize management.

Then, there was the fact that our work was fragmented into extremely specialized subcategories, for things like my work with Transit, or those who worked on residential high-rises, or bridge and tunnel work. It was also hard to categorize existing safety managers: the proposed union rules meant you going to pay a guy with 40 years of experience the same as a guy with ten. Finally, each one of us worked pretty much alone, with no chance to bring an apprentice up to speed since no contractor would pay for two site safety managers on a site. Heck, there were not even enough of us to go around!

Confessions of a Female Safety Engineer

But, in my opinion, the worst part of the proposal was that they would do exactly nothing to better our working conditions, but it would cut into our pay.

And my employer, gobsmacked as he was by this internal betrayal by one of his trusted supervisors, had to follow all the National Labor Relations Act rules. He not could interfere with the unionization process once it had begun. That would have been an Unfair Labor Practice under Section 8 of the NLRA, and they would haul him before the National Labor Relations Board. He could not fire the guy who was betraying him, either. He could not stop the unionization efforts, or hold meetings about the union in a supervisor's office. The vote was scheduled, and it went forward.

On the day of the union vote we all went in and had a nice little secret ballot. Terry met me outside of the voting area, serene in the fact that since everyone was polite to him, his new union boss status was in the bag.

But of our 107 employees, the only ones who voted for unionization were the three organizers who would have had jobs with the new union hierarchy. We did not want a union. We were happy as things were, thank you.

It was a crushing defeat, and those who had tried to pound such a square peg into a very round hole slunk off into early retirements - or to jobs with union halls, where they belonged.

BELLEVUE

ABOUT THIS TIME I WAS TRANSFERRED TO BELLEVUE HOSPITAL CENTER, NOW known as NYC Health + Hospitals/Bellevue. It's is a huge medical complex, with the best trauma room in lower Manhattan. This construction project involved a new outpatient clinic where the parking garage used to be, that was to be covered with a huge skylight over an atrium, so the windows that had faced the old parking lot would still receive light. We were also replacing the HVAC ducting in the core of the 21-story tower, known as the "cube," and were doing other upgrades: a new cooling tower, a new acute care floor, and two new chillers on one of the mechanical floors.

I was on this project for over two years. It was so spread out it really drove home the fact that I could only be responsible for the conditions when I was there, in that snapshot of time. But the biggest challenge was not that it was a huge job, some of it in a working hospital. The biggest challenge was that it was a DASNY job.

Ah, DASNY. The Dormitory Authority of the State of New York was in charge of all construction projects for the state of New York, usually hospitals and college work. They did not hire a General Contractor (GC), they hired what they called "Prime Contractors" for the major trades, and a Construction Manager (CM). This was a problem, for the GC would typically handle things like site cleanup and maintenance of things like safety railings and covering floor holes. My client, as the CM, became the defacto GC as far as maintaining safety on the site, but without any budget to do it! I suggested they work it into the change orders, as a percentage, and as there were many change orders that eventually worked.

Another problem with the site was that it was a hospital, and when guys even had a hangover, they went to the Emergency Room and tried to charge it to the job.

But the worst problem was the superintendent for one of the Prime Contractors, the one that handled the concrete, masonry and carpentry. I'd be early as usual and waiting around for the Job Progress meeting to start and he'd arrive and start being obnoxious. Remember this was all in front of five to ten other management reps. Mr. Obnoxious and I would have verbal sparring matches before the job progress meetings that sort of went like this.

He'd boast, in very bad taste, about his most recent sexual relationship, which was usually with a married woman so she'd not make any long-term demands on him, feel guilty and eventually break it off. Then he'd basically insinuate that I could be next. I'd cut him with a polite but devastating double *entendré* that had the other men wincing. The main reasons none of them stepped up with more than sympathetic looks was probably that I was handling him just fine on my own. It was quite an education to the decent men at the table about what women had to put up with! And you would think, as acerbic as my remarks were that the guy would stop, especially considering that he thought he was smart but my retorts made it obvious I was having a battle of wits with an unarmed man. But no.

This went on, once a week, for a couple of months until I complained to someone and they finally spoke to him. That merely slowed him down for a while. As I've already stated, I am not a litigious sort. But I asked my client's project manager to tell this man's boss that I was considering suing, and that finally put the kibosh on the abuse.

Note: Mr. Obnoxious was also had one of the worst safety attitudes I'd ever seen. Unprofessional behavior is rarely confined to one area of a person's life. I'd once dealt with a safety engineer on a site adjacent to the circuit breaker houses project who kept "borrowing" our rented scissor lifts and returning them covered with spattered paint. He was also a serial sexual harasser. Despite the shortage of people doing SSM work, he was let go.

Meanwhile, while I was at Bellevue, my immediate superior John was driving me nuts. He spent an incredible amount of time yelling at me for simple misunderstandings, and would not listen to any explanations. One common cause for his screaming lectures was, of all things, tool names. I'd call a tool by a name I'd heard, like a "hammer drill." But John thought I should use a different name, like "rotary hammer," which was in his opinion the *correct* name for the tool. And I would be told to "say what I meant" and yelled at for using the "wrong" tool name for 20 minutes. Trying to get a word in edgewise only made the screaming louder, and prolonged the agony.

It was not just me. One of the few other female safety managers I knew, Diane, had quit over his antics and gone elsewhere. So I started looking for another job as a consulting safety manager, too. The situation had become intolerable.

Tall Boys, Steamfitters, and Chill

One of our contractors at Bellevue, a steamfitter company, had run into financial problems. I shared an office with the man from the bonding company who was helping them finish their work. The steamfitters had every incentive to cut corners, and I constantly caught them doing insane things like having a very overweight worker sit on inadequate counterweights when they were hoisting up a heavy item. He bobbed on that unsecured thing like a dunking stool, while his boss was poised to go out on a ledge past the safety railing without fall protection to check on what was being hoisted. They nearly got thrown off the site several times.

This next story is not unrelated. One Monday I came in to discover the site in an uproar, and the Bellevue hospital "cube" building with no air conditioning on what was going to be a warm day. Many of the patients in what would become a hot environment without A/C—in places like the neonatal ward with all its machines—were about to be transferred to nearby NYU Hospital. And supposedly it was all our fault. To which we said, "Huh?"

There had been a major safety issue on Saturday night going into Sunday morning, when one of the hospital's chillers quit working. Bellevue has four chillers; two old ones, one we just installed and turned over for their use, and one the steamfitters were adding. My friend Michael the mechanical engineer had gotten a midnight call from the hospital mechanical room; the chiller we had just turned over to them was down. Did he have the number for York maintenance? Despite the hour, Michael called his York construction division contact and he got them the emergency maintenance number. He did ask the hospital maintenance folks, "Are any of our men there?" They said no.

In fact, what had happened was this. The steamfitter company had been unable to afford their mens' union benefits, called stamps, and the union men would not work until they had caught up. The man who ran the company was boxed in, as he needed these men to work or he'd lose his house and his business to the bonding company.

125

Confessions of a Female Safety Engineer

New York State law had a loophole where you could hire workers who were not in a union but paid at a union rate, and the hospital had some paid-by-union-scale steamfitters on call. Our desperate steamfitter company boss had asked for these steamfitters' phone numbers and called them in.

When the Bellevue maintenance supervisor from that shift saw the union-scale steamfitters they employed from time to time, he assumed that the previous Bellevue maintenance shift had called them in and not that these men were working for an outside company.

It got worse. Whatever they had done, these steamfitters eventually knocked out the new chiller *and* the old ones. Once Bellevue maintenance had called the company that had a contract to keep the new chiller running, a technician came to the hospital. One of the old chillers only needed him to throw a circuit breaker. The tech then used a regular voltage tester on the other, 600-volt system, on a machine clearly marked "HIGH VOLTAGE." The tester blew up in his hands, permanently damaging his hearing and causing burns on his face, neck and arms. The explosion also knocked out the hospital's one working old chiller.

We got people in and got their chillers working again in a few hours, so no one had to be evacuated to nearby NYU Hospital. And in one of the more intricate incident investigations I'd ever done, in a single afternoon my client and I pieced together the timeline above, and braced for a visit from our insurance auditor on the next day.

Now, understand that my client, like most large construction firms, was self-insured. A big insurer like AIG, Liberty Mutual, or Wausau would come in and advise them how much their cash reserves should be, which was money set aside to pay out in case of projected accidents. And for about 3% of those reserves, they'd allow the use of their insurance license and monitor the safety on the site. This 3% paid for monthly safety-audits of that self-insured contractor's job. Another part of their service was to help us prepare for lawsuits. This one looked like it was going to be a doozy.

Our defense, I decided, had three important points.

1. **Breach of contract**. The Steamfitter subcontractor did not tell us he was coming in after hours. I got a copy of the safety clause in this client's contracts, which is not something safety engineers normally

126

do, I'm told, but I always did that with a new client. Since all subs were required to tell the contractor when they have men working after regular hours so that oversight could be provided, not notifying my client that they were doing work after hours was a breach of contract.

2. **Lack of Training.** I suggested they ask for copies of the training documentation for the technician who was called in. I provided photos of the numerous DANGER, HIGH VOLTAGE signs that he ignored when he used a low-voltage tester. He knew, or should have known, that a high voltage system needed a high voltage tester. Further, he had not been wearing proper safety gear which exacerbated his injuries. Where were his safety training records?

3. **Unreliable chiller.** One of the existing chillers that supposedly went out when the steamfitters were welding was an older model that had a history of going out on them. I suggested they subpoena the Bellevue maintenance log book for that mechanical room.

Everyone told me this would be going to court in a few years. I was advised to make a file because they would call me in as a witness, so I did. But I never was called in. The insurance rep told me I basically laid out the entire legal strategy for them to defend my client in my recommendations, and I later learned they'd used my strategy. The insurance rep wished all safety managers would make his job so easy. I checked a few years later, and my client was ruled not at all responsible.

This brings up an important aspect of my work. Everything I did at as a safety manager was to protect three entities: the company, the workers, and myself. Each simple safety training session that I documented told a later court, if there is one, that I and the company I represented *told* that person not to do whatever it was; they signed that they knew it was wrong and they did it anyhow. This lowered the percentage of liability for my client or company. When an employer is self-insured that can mean the difference between them going out of business or making a profit on a job.

I was proud to be a part of protecting this client who was so proactive on handling safety matters. They should not have been in any way legally responsible for the negligence of others, done behind their backs.

Confessions of a Female Safety Engineer

⚠

Meanwhile, the steamfitter company somehow stayed in business, don't ask me how other than the fact that the wheels of justice tend to grind slowly. And they were still on my site.

You'd think they'd have learned their lesson from the whole chillers debacle, but you'd be wrong. Soon after the incident with the chillers they again stayed late without informing us. They thought they were hidden. I, who'd read the detailed computerized construction schedule, knew what they were slated to work on next, and checked that remote location anyhow.

I found them, working after hours without informing us (*again*), in a mechanical room on the top of the new outpatient clinic, a room with walls to shield it from wind but no roof; this allowed my client to bring any heavy HVAC equipment in and out via crane. The steamfitters were in there with three six packs of tall-boy beers: one six-pack was empty and one six-pack was half gone. The men who'd consumed the beers were also half-gone, and were nevertheless welding. To add insult to injury, they were doing this permit-required hot work without a permit.

I think they knew the jig was up, but they argued with me. And I did not take this as them not listening to me as a woman. I took it as them desperately stalling to put off the inevitable. I, personally, did not pay their company, but my client did. So I just went out and called my buddy Michael the mechanical engineer to deal with them. He got there in record time, and they were finally ordered off our site.

Six months later I saw the same crew later at another jobsite, not laid off but working. Throwing someone off your site for a safety violation was not something that ended their work, it ended just their work on that particular project.

I have no idea what happened to the company who had a problem with the bonding company. Its owner might have squeaked through, he might not have.

I suspect not.

An End, And the Start
of Mandatory Overtime

I WROTE EARLIER OF MY MOTHER'S ILLNESS, THAT SHE WAS ON DIALYSIS. THE stress of working plus being her caregiver was so bad that project management one time caught me sleeping in a pile of tarps, and they were sympathetic enough to let it slide. It was a hell where I was lucky to get three or four hours of sleep a night if her treatment ran late. Then she passed away, and Consulting Inc. not only sent flowers to the funeral but gave me an extra week of paid compassionate leave.

Once my mother died, things changed. Mind you, the company was great to me, but her illness and my rushing home three nights a week to get her to dialysis had shielded me from something that was in some ways far worse: mandatory overtime.

Up until this point I'd had a modicum of life balance. It helped that I am one of those people who only needs six hours of sleep a night, and I was organized. So life was good. I was active in my church, where I sang in the choir, played my guitar in the church band, and helped run the emergency food pantry. I was able to spend time with my sons, and had time for editing an online magazine and writing. But from this time forward until I retired, I worked at least 55-hour weeks. When you added in the commute they were more like 70-hour weeks. It was insane. I worked every Saturday, and every other Sunday, but learned to refuse more than that because I invariably got sick from that much overwork.

It started when a piece of heavy equipment on an adjacent construction site fell into an empty chamber from a buried building that would not support its weight. This acted like an excavation without any structural protections next to Bellevue's old admin building, and a crack went up the admin building's outer wall, from the foundation to the roof. Worse, the roof joists were no longer aligned with the columns and the whole building was structurally at risk.

The emergency solution, once they'd removed the heavy equipment from the hole, was to fill the pit it had fallen into, and then cut and raise the admin

Confessions of a Female Safety Engineer

wall columns in the basement with heavy-duty hydraulic jacks until the columns met the roof joists again. Although it was an admin building, it was next to a hospital full of sick people. Until they saw how much noise and vibration that work made it had to be done carefully, and they tested it on the night shift. I was tasked with staying until maybe 11 or 12 in the morning with a 7 AM start time the next day. Since it was 2 hours each way to home and back, I called my now-teen sons and slept that first night on the floor, which earned me the grudging sobriquet "tough broad" from my nemesis supervisor, John.

Subsequent nights I brought a change of clothes and a reclining beach lounge chair to sleep on that after the work was done. Overtime was nice, but I was so tired I would only kick off my construction boots and fall asleep fully clothed more times than not. This sort of schedule went on for years. Thank God my work was fascinating, or I'd have quit over the hours alone.

⚠

Not all the stresses were the fault of my hours. One time there was a man run over in front of our site, on 2nd Avenue. There was an ambulance headed uptown that was pushing a semi truck full of heavy sand to run a red light and let it through, and the truck driver did so right when some poor man was dashing across the street. It happened at lunch time, and fell to me to see if it was one of our workers. I just had the police lift the tarp enough show me the flattened man's shoes. Sneakers, not construction boots? Whew. Not one of our men.

Then there was the case of the "hammer lady." Remember that contractor's superintendent that was a font of sexual innuendo? He'd done or said things that had a very attractive black worker actually blackmailing him via threat of a lawsuit to keeping her working until the job was done. When the project was completed, they had to lay her off and she went bonkers. She literally took up a hammer and single handedly destroyed a recently-finished cinderblock wall, and then went through that wall and used her hammer on thousands of dollars worth of tools in their tool room.

I was tasked with keeping an eye on her after she left the building. I was supposedly on the line with a friend for the hot dog cart while she waited just outside the job for her "car service," which in NYC parlance was like a taxi you called for rather than hailed: a discrete unmarked, limo-like car. While she waited she was still clutching her hammer, and screaming into her cell phone. We really wondered if she'd do bodily harm to someone but she kept her rage solely confined to property damage. And they dared not prosecute her.

It was alarming, but in a way very fitting that the subcontractor that would not rein in a serial sexual harasser, and my client who should have brought the figurative legal hammer down, had to suffer *some* sort of penalty for that omission. Everything an attractive younger woman goes through on a construction site is not necessarily about sex but *damn* if she did not have a point.

In this, I was perhaps lucky for I started in the construction industry when I was in my mid-thirties and worked in it until my mid fifties. I considered it a plus that I was not young or what most people would consider all that good looking. I was no raging beauty. Therefore I'd come to a conscious decision years ago that since modern standards of beauty were not attainable for me? The hell with it. I strove to be well groomed, neatly dressed, and healthy and not give a flying hoot what others thought about my so-called "looks."

The flip side of not being insulted by being treated as a gorgeous sex object was to be insulted by being treated as an ugly older woman, someone who might be an 'easy score' because she was probably desperate. Since I had consciously made the decision to be asexual for a while, that also slid off me like water off a duck's back. I'm not saying it was not hurtful, but it was easier to ignore it than to prosecute these creeps or let them think it was getting to me. They wanted to play power games over sex? Fine. I had *real power* as the person who could get them written up for their unsafe actions, or walk off their site when there was a shortage of people in my profession and my absence might shut down their job. While I would not misuse that power it was there. And they damned well knew it.

That's what it meant to be a trailblazer. I often call myself an accidental feminist because I did not consciously set out to become a highly successful woman in a traditionally male job, but that's what happened. It's one thing to believe in equal pay for equal work, but quite another to make that happen.

The next step in making that happen was finishing my degree. I'd gone through my graduation ceremony years ago, lacking only three credits, which were supposed to be finished as the second part of a two-part work study.

Confessions of a Female Safety Engineer

Taking care of my ailing mother had taken my focus off that for a while. And then, despite repeated requests, the head of the consulting company I worked for had no time to help me with the work study, and my supervisor John sure wasn't about to!

Toward the end of the Bellevue job I received notice that Mercy College had rescinded the first three credits of my two-part work-study and I was now *six* credits from my degree. So as I packed for the next site, I looked around for alternative courses they would accept. I found two at the University of Connecticut, both online courses, and I applied to have my employer pay for my last six credits. They said yes.

THE FINAL SIX CREDITS
& FORT KNOX

I SPENT THE NEXT SEVERAL MONTHS ON THE TAIL END OF A REALLY INTERESTING project in Brooklyn: the NYC Transit Revenue Center, nicknamed Fort Knox. The place would eventually handle six million dollars a day in cash and Metrocards. I was able to write some papers for my UCONN Safety & Security online course about the things I learned there. Somehow, despite the long hours I worked, I finished my two online summer courses and those credits were forwarded to Mercy College for approval.

Meanwhile, "Fort Knox" was truly amazing. On the ultra secure side of the parking lot, toward the loading docks, vehicles were slated to drive into the area through a place where a guard booth would eventually have cameras looking under the vehicle, while driver and vehicle were penned in like cattle in a feedlot by steel gates in front and behind then. Vehicles being inspected could not back out without puncturing their tires.

All of the tall, razor-wire-topped fences around the perimeter of the site had fine mesh with sensors sensitive enough to know if a squirrel was climbing up them; they had little weather stations every so often so it could allow for the wind and rain. Similar sensors were on the roof.

The trucks that brought in the cash were armored and had armed guards, and they went into individual loading bays, each with another two-step security setup. The trucks were locked into closed sections with airlock-like secondary pass-through corridors where they made sure whoever was driving or riding shotgun was not someone who could compromise the whole facility.

The office section housed the security cameras. It was like what I imagine a Vegas casino's security would have to be: 360° cameras over each person making and working with Metrocards, cameras on the room that sorted change from huge bins into quarters, nickels and dimes, cameras over the people who worked with bundles of cash...cameras everywhere.

I really liked that I was able to park on this site, and for free; so many jobs were only accessible via an exhausting commute on the Long Island Railroad, plus bus or subway, or you'd best drive but had to pay anywhere from $12 to $15 a day to park. And there were no bridge or tunnel tolls needed to get there, which was another relief to my budget. I was still paying off student loans, and still had two teen sons to support. Every little bit helped. Despite getting a $5K a year raise due to the coming degree, I was still making $15K a year less than my male co-workers. And that was unacceptable.

What was funny was I had a better grip on what my time was worth to my employer than some of my male co-workers had about their value. I'd run a business, and I knew that as a rough gauge you paid employees half of what they cost you. So if a worker cost you $50 an hour he or she got $25 an hour before taxes. This covered everything from taxes employees never see, insurance, and equipment like cell phones or computers. But we were consultants; we were the *product* our boss was selling. A product is sold for at twice what it costs a business: to cover cost of goods, overhead, and profit. So when my company charged $125/hr for a consultant, and that person costs them $66/hr he should be bringing home about $33 an hour. I actually met a male coworker who was let go because he was constantly badmouthing the boss as a crook: he'd seen that the boss was charging the client four times what he made per hour, and he thought he was being ripped off.

My employer was charging our customers over five times what I made per hour. Maybe the boss did not know that I was aware of this imbalance, but I was. With as many jobs as I covered, seeing his contract with some of our clients was inevitable

After working at "Fort Knox" all day, I'd often be set to cover another transit job on the way home. At least the scheduler tried to keep these on my driving route, but the hours were brutal. I'd leave the house at 5 AM at the latest and usually not be home until 10 or 11 at night. I got into the habit of ordering my groceries online, picking them up on Sundays, and cooking ahead for a week or two and freezing it. I also had a stash of "too tired to cook" processed foods but tried not to use them.

One time I was called for jury duty. I wanted to do this. Heck, it would have been like a *vacation*. But my boss had me excused as "critical personnel" since my absence would have thrown 200-300 men out of work when there was no one to be the legally mandated site safety manager on a site.

Wendy S. Delmater

I got in the habit of carrying Zicam tablets in my purse, in case I felt the least bit sick. You think a *mother* cannot be sick? Try being a mother AND "critical personnel."

Again, thank God I loved my work. I don't think I would have survived it otherwise.

SHARPEN YOUR PENCIL
WHILE AT SCHOOL CONSTRUCTION

THE NEXT JOB THEY SENT ME TO WAS EVEN DEEPER INTO BROOKLYN, A combination elementary and middle school that was replacing an old burned out city block in Brownsville. It revitalized the neighborhood, and was a project I was proud to be a part of. It was , however, my first experience in dealing with the incredibly dysfunctional NYC School Construction Authority, the SCA.

I cannot even begin to describe what a mess the SCA was but I can hint at it by saying those who even bothered to bid on SCA jobs routinely added 30 percent to their bids as an annoyance factor. Almost no one who worked in SCA project management had any construction experience. These were either political payoff jobs, or the worst possible use of affirmative action: putting people who were not even remotely qualified into key positions solely on the basis of their gender, race, or ethnicity. Many of the SCA construction management people at least tried to get it right, and I was more than willing to help them. But there was a lot of power-tripping going on, and there were a lot of ridiculous and arbitrary rules. Their safety director was intellectual lightweight screamer who had left OSHA to join SCA but she could not climb ladders to inspect things: they were only rated up to 350 pounds.

The contractors who bothered to do SCA work were not top-tier, either. My client's lead superintendent, for example, absolutely refused to wear a hard hat in the field. (I did manage to get him to at least carry it so he could say "I just took it off" to any inspectors.) Still, it was a pretty safe site. I had the usual arguments with those who did not want to do and turn in weekly safety meetings, MSDS sheets, and site orientations, but I kept those firmly in line.

I enjoyed exploring the neighborhood on breaks. Lunch at *Po Boy's Fish and Take* was always fun.

The crisis came when the SCA sent down a ruling from on high that despite it only being the 6-month "training period" before a new OSHA steel erection standard went into legal effect, they wanted the standard enacted on their sites *now*. The steel workers on my site adamantly refused to cooperate. They'd bid the

Confessions of a Female Safety Engineer

job based on the old standard, still in effect, and that was how they were going to finish it. After three weeks of this wrangling, OSHA showed up and did a cursory look at the site, and then zeroed in on the steel erectors, trying like mad things to fine them for anything. I heartily suspected that the SCA's insane safety director called up one of her old OSHA buddies and asked them to give us hell.

They went straight for the easiest, most common fines: recordkeeping. But the OSHA inspectors trying to rake the steel erectors over the coals were frustrated: all the steel erector's recordkeeping for things like safety training, MSDSs, and safety orientations were all in perfect order. The steel erectors worshiped the ground I walked on after that inspection, because my work had saved them tens of thousands of dollars in fines.

Most safety engineers are reduced to nail-biting (if not a gibbering panic) by such an experience. But this was not my first OSHA inspection. Remember the 2.5 month videotaped OSHA inspection on my first safety job? This time OSHA was there for part of one day, and then left. That was child's play compared to my earlier experience. So I wrote up a report on what happened, stating both the facts, the timeline, the conclusion, and my suspicions about who had sent them, and emailed it to my boss. Then I went to a gym to swim due to a rare lack of overtime work. I left my cell phone in the car.

When I came out, I found a panicked voicemail from my company's big boss. I called him back and suggested he look at his email for my report. I was sorry I had missed his call. I'd been at the gym.

"At the...gym. You're already sent a report? And you're not upset?" my boss asked, incredulous.

I reminded him this was not my first OSHA inspection, and gave him a précis of what happened, again suggesting he read my report. The inspectors were just people who put on their pants one leg at a time and I ran very safe sites, so what was the problem? I hung up, asking myself, *Was my confidence and experience that unusual? Then why couldn't I find a better job?*

Frankly, I was disgusted with the job search. I kept getting enthusiastic we'll-hire-you! first interviews and then was passed over. I suspected that the old NJ contractor was still giving me a very bad reference and one of the many recruiters who kept calling me confirmed that this was true. So I made a way around that.

138

A man who was now a co-worker and a friend had worked for the NJ contractor during the same time period, and with his permission I put *his* phone number on my resume as a reference for the NJ employer, stating that of all the people from that time period when I was on those sites, he was the only one that was "still available." It was true; the NJ contractor was only going by old records.

And I was accepted by the next place I applied to, a firm that did almost nothing but NYC Transit projects, and for a salary my work and experience should have commanded. I called employer's big boss to give him my two week's notice. I offered to pay him back for my recent college courses. I explained that I could not live on what he was paying me.

My boss was shocked. "You just had a yearly evaluation with us. Why didn't you say you couldn't live on what we were paying you then?" he wanted to know.

"Because you said that was all you could afford, and I was stupid enough to believe you," I replied with quiet heat.

He asked if I would allow him to sharpen his pencil, and make a counter-offer.

Warily, I said yes.

His counter-offer was a base pay of $15K more per year, balanced by my overtime not kicking in until I'd worked 10 hours a day, and then only time-and-a-half for overtime, even on Sundays. I accepted.

And upon hearing the news of my taking the counter-offer, my old supervisor John finally stopped being snide with me. I had a degree now. I had proved that could leave. And I'd negotiated like a confident adult with the guy who ran the company, his boss. There was new respect from John and all of the management team above me.

I bought a small bottle of champagne. I'd earned equal pay and treatment as a female, at last.

Tales out of School

SINCE I HAD PROVED I COULD HANDLE THE SCA, I GOT QUITE A FEW school construction jobs after that. One of them was in Queens, a huge multi-school project off the Cross Island Expressway where they were building two elementary schools and a middle school on the same campus. This job was just going into the cold season, so I had my first encounter with the intricacies of providing temporary heat to a project.

Most jobs start construction in the very early spring and try to get the interiors enclosed before winter hits. That means finishing the walls, roof, and windows. Even if you don't have a boiler yet, you'll at least have an interior to work on that is not leaking heat to the elements or subject to rain and snow.

This site, no doubt due to it being an SCA job, had missed that deadline, and we went through a winter where the window openings and doors were covered with tarps or plastic sheeting. It takes a lot more heat to make such a leaking sieve of a building warm enough for masons to work—they were adding cinderblock walls and tile—but that's what they had to do. They got the requisite permits from the Fire Department of the New York City (FDNY) and rented huge propane heaters. An enormous protected area was set aside for propane tank storage, and that storage had to be permitted by FNDY, too. All sorts of warning signage and tank-moving precautions had to be observed. People had to have "fire watch" training permits, also from FDNY.

This is on top of all the things I had to do as a safety manager with a three-building, multi-story site to walk. Temp heat was like a large project within the project. And it was still pretty chilly in those structures—I envied my youngest son who'd just moved to Florida—but the brick and block went up.

A note about those bricks: they were genius. To make the walls in the schools bright, cheerful, easy to clean, and graffiti-proof, they used bricks that had been glazed with bright, shiny colors on one side. This also meant there was no painting expense for the interior walls: not as new construction, and not maintenance painting. I was very impressed.

141

Confessions of a Female Safety Engineer

We eventually installed the windows in the spring and summer, once the temporary heat was no longer needed. Better late than never.

Another SCA job l I worked on was in the Bronx, just off the Whitestone Bridge. This school had just had all the asbestos that had been encapsulated removed during the summer, and they were now doing lead removal before the kids came back. Talk about touchy work! There are whole sets of rules for dealing with asbestos in a school near kids, and rightly so. I was just as glad to come in on the lead abatement side of things: I had a lot of experience in lead abatement work, especially with transit.

I did work with potential asbestos encapsulation in one school, but that was outside of NYC. It was potentially that worst-case blue asbestos boiler insulation, and the protection around the boiler was ripped. I had to get that school checked by an asbestos firm; when I supervised one of those, it meant making sure the potentially contaminated air was under pressure so it could not escape unless it went through a special HEPA filter. The airlock going in and out of the contaminated area, with showers, was multiple chambers, and I inspected it before it was used – right down to the soap. There were required signs all around the decontamination area, required permits (even more needed in NYC than outside of the City) and I had to make sure the workers were trained. All of their safety gear had to be inspected, including respirators.

Asbestos abatement was not one of my favorite things to do. What was worse, in my opinion, was that the crews that did asbestos abatement in the NY area were all eastern European, usually Polish, and smoked like chimneys; smoking hugely increased their risk of lung cancer when working with asbestos. But that's who signed up to do the job.

I made sure all the other risk factors were taken care of, but smokers doing asbestos removal was about as sane as diabetics working in a candy factory. It was not a good environment for them.

I did the best I could. They'd all been medically cleared to do the work, and been personally fit-tested for respirator work by me. At the end of the job I boxed up their medical records which would have to be stored for 30 years, and prayed that no unscrupulous employer would have a convenient fire that somehow destroyed those records.

I prayed for them and hoped for jobs for myself in the open air.

Bronx Rail Yard
Near Manhattan College

I WAS NEXT SENT TO A HUGE ELEVATED NYC TRANSIT RAIL YARD WITH PARKING underneath, up on the edge of Westchester County, in the Bronx. I suspected it was not just my up-to-date track training with NYC Transit that got me this job; a lot of my fellow safety managers refused work in the Bronx since the $180 in month tolls on the Throgs Neck Bridge or the Whitestone Bridge were not reimbursable; they were considered a commuting expense. I took it in stride, and always went where they sent me except for the one time a new scheduler tied to send me to dangerous Bedford Stuyvesant on a night shift. I would not have even taken that position with two armed guards at my side.

But this was a nice neighborhood near Manhattan College. The parking area under the elevated train yard had bad drainage, and the steel columns that held up the yard were in very moist soil and rusting. The job involved a lot of lead paint removal, with all that entailed, plus steel and concrete to reinforce the pillar bases, and painting. Painting around high-voltage electrified rails was a special treat. How high was the voltage? The wires feeding each third rail had to be split into four two-inch thick feeders to be thin enough to even *bend*.

One of the challenges of this job was that the company which won the bid was run by someone from India. Many of his painters were Punjabi, and the lead paint removal crew was Polish. Their foremen spoke English, but their men did not. So I had to do safety meetings with a translator. Of course, I had no idea what the foremen were telling their men in their own language. A trick there was to embed a joke in the training. If all the men laughed at the joke, the translator was doing his job.

We also had union protests outside the site. As I mentioned earlier, New York state allows non-union work as long as you pay "union scale" wages, and my client was paying union scale, but the unions wanted real union painters. Nevertheless, the protests were kind of futile, mainly since they were picketing on a poorly-travelled street on the backside of nowhere. The protest dwindled to one lonely guy with holding placard for about a month, and then they gave up.

Confessions of a Female Safety Engineer

But my client still had a couple of union men on site, who'd come with the light stands. You know those big nighttime lights on poles attached to generators you see when contractors are doing overnight highway work? The contractor had rented several of them, at $500 a month, because it was November and got dark early. Heck, it was dark under the tracks to begin with. In New York, renting those machines alerted the unions that they needed to be attended by a union Mechanic, and a union Oiler.

The Mechanic's sole duty was to turn the light stands on an off, but not to repair them. The Oiler fueled the light stands; no one else was allowed to do this simple chore. They charged exorbitant rates for this level of "service." I quietly suggested to the superintendent that the light stands were causing shadows for the lead paint removal crew and the painters working in their scissor lifts, and wouldn't it be safer to use those little halogen light rigs you could buy at Home Depot for $30 each, set right up there inside the scissor lifts? It would save them money. The super could even take credit for my money-saving idea.

The super bought some small halogen lights and some extension cords, returned the big light stands to the rental company, and send the union Mechanic and Oiler packing. He got a raise for "his" brilliant idea, and for the rest of the job I could do no wrong.

"Wendy really knows her stuff. Whatever she says to do about safety, do it!"

Safety, if done correctly, will save a company money. This was one of the best examples of me teaching that. And now, this superintendent owed me, big time, and was happy to follow the safety rules, especially when I explained how each one of them saved him even more money in some way.

Once a contractor understands *that*, the rest is just cleanup. I worked on and off on vacation relief for other safety managers when this client was working in bus yards for NYC Transit, and on other subway work. From that point on, I could see that they "got" it. They were converted. They understood that Safety Pays.

Bronx Rail Yard near White Plains, and a Flapper

When I was done with the Manhattan College Yard, there was another transit job in the Bronx. This one was at a rail yard, too – the 241st Street Yard. The contractor was removing fire hydrants in the midst of the yard. These hydrants' locations made sense before the rails were electrified, but were useless now that you'd have to drag a wet fire hose over electrified rails to use them. The new hydrants were to go along the access road.

Early in my tenure there, I was in on a job progress meeting in Transit's main offices at 2 Broadway where I set my posture, with humor.

You see, there were two 100-foot-tall fire suppression towers in the middle of the yard, which looked approximately like metal forest ranger towers, but with literal cannons on top. I'm not saying they were old, but after the Civil War, a brass cannon maker switched to making water cannons and these were from that time period. The NYC Transit representative at the meeting tried to sound totally reasonable when he suggested that these were "hydrants" to be removed, covered by my client's contract.

The client, dumbfounded and angry was about to mount a defense when I remarked, dryly. "That's a hydrant? I'd like to see the dog." In the choked silence that followed, the client relaxed and smiled. The transit rep quietly squirmed, and dropped the subject.

The client and I got along fine after that. The neighborhood had a community garden where I spent my lunch breaks. After very long days where I at least enjoying a bit of gardening on my breaks, I came home gifted with basil, peppers, or tomatoes.

Perhaps the most important thing that happened on that site was how I was able to protect my client in a dispute. Understand that most of New York City's rail system is so old that they have no "as built" plans, and if even if you try to call before you dig, they cannot tell you where anything is. They literally don't know. Then, if you hit something underground, they charge you for replacing whatever you hit.

Confessions of a Female Safety Engineer

As far as Transit was concerned, there was no downside for this. They got free upgrades and they'd have "as built" plans that you paid for, too. Indeed, Transit seemed to go out of their way to try and get contractors to pay for things by blaming them. Our best defense, and a huge part of my job, was to take a lot of digital photos: before, during. and after our work.

The main danger excavating in any train yard was taking out signal wires; they were everywhere and fragile, and cutting one could cause a train to crash. And they were low voltage, so unlike high voltage lines they had no protective plates above them to warn you. I took a lot of pictures to show how careful my client was digging near a known signal location to put in his new hydrant pipes. There was no heavy equipment involved. He did it all by hand, with shovels, by the book per OSHA, carefully securing a proper ladder for the men to get in and out of the excavation. I took numerous photos of the unearthed signal wires, carefully worked around and intact.

One time the signal went out anyhow, and because we were working in the area we were blamed by Transit. At the inquiry, as evidence, they had a photo of the "signal wires" being hit by our ladder. I had pretty much the same photo on my laptop, and enlarged it so they could all see that the so-called signal wire in their photo was a piece of nine-gauge wire, like you use to tie rebar together in a concrete forms, being used to secure the ladder to wooden stakes so it would not shift. 9-wire is less than a 16th of an inch thick and not insulated. I showed them another photo of the signal wires we'd dug around and protected; these were three-quarters of an inch in diameter, and had black insulation.

My client was ruled not responsible for the signal outage.

During this project, I got some sad news. Aunt Anna, my children's grand great aunt on their father's side, had died. We went to her funeral, full of lovely memories about her and her husband. She'd been a flapper, and did industrial safety during WWII. She'd also helped the family with money she inherited from her uncle, who'd worked in Thomas Edison's lab. Her husband had flown Air Force One for Truman and Eisenhower, then been a farmer for 20 years, then a lay chaplain at the local VA and public hospitals. My children idolized the man.

She'd left me a few mementos, but all the other relatives had gone through their house ahead of me. I went through her jewelry box and amid the cheap

146

trinkets I found a broken men's ring and a broken string of pearls. *People*, I said to myself, *do not keep broken costume jewelry*. The necklace turned out to be Aunt Anna's real cultured pearls, which I had restrung. The ring turned out to be a phenomenal find. It was Uncle Marvin's gold graduation ring, with an enormous real aquamarine, I had it repaired, and when I eventually got my college diploma it became my college graduation ring.

I thought that was all I would receive, but several months later I discovered she'd left me enough to pay off my student loans, my credit card, and my car loan. Everyone who knew I'd inherited a good amount of money wondered why I did not go out and buy a new car, but I just had my Hyundai detailed. Unexpected things will happen. I wanted to have some savings to fall back on. I continued to be frugal. I even carpooled to my next job, but then at that time gas was $4 a gallon.

Staten Island Ferry

I WAS ASSIGNED TO A PROJECT THAT WAS PART OF ENLARGING THE #1 LINE, #5 line and W subway station by the Staten Island Ferry terminal. The ferries were also owned by NYC Transit since they connected the Manhattan subways and busses to the Staten Island Rail. Since this new project was affected by the ocean I carpooled in with a dockworker, and kept the hours of the tides. Another savings: unlike a lot of jobs there was a free parking at this site. But that was an artifact of 9/11; the bus station under part of the terminal had been deemed too big a risk for a car bomb so they turned it into limited parking. I was part of the management team so I got one of the coveted parking spaces.

I came in toward the end of this project. The job was winding down. Things were not supposed to be very dangerous.

I'd been here before, on vacation relief, back when it was dangerous and they were erecting steel over the water, which had a unique set of challenges including deepwater vests and rescue boats. One day I'd climbed up to the top of the steel they were erecting, to check on the iron workers. As I suspected, they were only feigning being tied off. The lanyards were for show, and attached to nothing.

I'd waved to their foreman. "Good morning! Wow, I see so much right going on up here! You're all wearing hard hats and safety glasses and deep water vests and more. So close to perfect. It would be really perfect if you tied off; looks like you forgot to after break." They had not forgotten, and they knew that I knew that. But they complied, surprised by the stream of compliments. And I stayed up there since, I told them, it was such a lovely morning and I was enjoying the view. It really was a lovely morning, but they knew I was watching them like a hawk. If a polite fiction kept them safe, that was fine with me.

And it *had been* a lovely morning; the vista included the Statue of Liberty, lots of boats, the Brooklyn docks, and Governor's Island. It sure beat the view when I'd recently spent all day watching roofers from the top of a fifteen-foot extension ladder, working on the station on a platform 150 feet above Broadway for the 1, 2, and 3 lines' train station in lower Harlem.

Confessions of a Female Safety Engineer

Returning now that this job when it was nearly completed meant I at least knew how to get there. And my bosses at the consulting company made no bones about me mainly being there to straighten out the records after an elderly safety manager, who was less than organized, retired. He had left a mess. In between walking the site on inspections I did the best I could, going through one box after other of the disorganized records, trying to make them coherent in case of future possible lawsuits. I began to feel like I was picking up a lazy child's toys. Why could they not do it themselves?

But there were compensations. The site had archeologists who were digging up NYC's past from the landfill the site was built on. There were boats and a sea breeze, and I got to see rare birds like a black-crested night heron near the dock, or a sleepy Eastern screech owl passed out on the hood of my car. The terminal was in a beautiful part of NYC, too, very near the South Street Seaport, where I went after work to events that interested me, if I could find the time. It was near great restaurants and a branch of the Smithsonian, and a farmer's market once a week. I glimpsed Richard Gere on the steps of the Smithsonian when they were filming a movie there, but seeing a movie crew in NYC was normal: the Brooklyn Navy Yard had become a warren of film studios and the old Silvercup Bread factory was now Silvercup Studios. New York was overtaking Hollywood, as I watched.

There was even a World Coffee location near the ferry terminal, a chain I loved when I consulted at the two towers before 9/11. I went there expecting just coffee and pleasant memories, but the taste and smell triggered flashbacks of the horror of 9/11. No, I was not over the trauma.

As for the job being safe? Instead I ran into one of the deadliest situations in my entire career as a safety manager.

They were excavating for storm drains on a late shift, in an area that had been cleared to excavate when the contractor had called to have the utility lines "marked out." They had still run into a problem. Was that a steam line they'd nicked? NYC has a lot of steam lines; the waste steam from the power plants heat a lot of homes and businesses in the winter. If so, it was not high pressure steam leak.

One of the men pulled me aside and said he was going home and calling in a junior person to take the rap. That was a POWER line they'd hit; the steam was from high-voltage electricity interacting with the moisture in the soil. It might explode at any time.

He left. I called Con Ed and tried to mitigate any potential harm to my men and the site if it blew. They got it fixed, and it did not explode, but it was a close one. After that, going through old boxes of records for my boss was positively relaxing.

This was not the only time I was asked to order the insanely bad records for a job after a slob had left. There was a 'mixed use' building on Central Park South, with its "skating rink" and televised drunk ironworkers that was worse.

MIXED USE, AND MUSIC

THERE WERE TWO JOBS I WORKED ON AS VACATION RELIEF THAT WERE RIGHT next to each other. First I spent a month at a mixed use—residential and commercial—high rise project that had been in the news a few months before my arrival. Investigative reporters had followed ironworkers to a bar where they ate lunch, and downed boilermakers. Then they went back to work, quite drunk. It was all caught on film, and was a huge story on television news. It was a scandal, and the insurer almost cancelled the general contractor's policy over it. Things were still tense.

I did the usual things: read the floor plans, walk the building, make a contact list of supposedly key personnel, and another list with cell phone numbers of the hidden hierarchy of those who actually got things done.

My walk-through revealed a very, very safe site. My guide pointed out where they'd had rainwater freeze all over a large part of an upper floor last winter; everyone still called the area "the skating rink."

I chipped away at trying to deal with the badly preserved and written site safety records. I did the best I could but it was putting lipstick on a pig; I could only pretend make that mess attractive to a helpful lawyer.

I had a problem with the site management, too. After all the mess with the investigative reporters and their insurance company, one of the management team came back from a three-martini lunch with alcohol on his breath. Now there is that rule: *you don't write up your client.* But I could not let that stand. So here is what I did.

Just before the big job progress meeting, I reported to the GC's project manager that I had seen a "drunk guy" come into the site, right past the security guard. He railed on and on during the meeting about how we had to be diligent about stopping that sort of thing. Can I help it if he pictured some sort of homeless guy as the drunk? After the meeting, but before he had a chance to yell at the security guard company, I quietly let him know it had been someone in that room, part of his management team.

Confessions of a Female Safety Engineer

I let *him* figure out who it was and let *him* write the guy up or fire him. The hazard was reported subtly to the client, the client was aware (and horrified), and the client would quietly deal with it. Mission accomplished.

⚠

The last "correct the records" job they sent me to was at the final stages of the *Jazz at Lincoln Center* project, about four blocks north and at the base of Central Park West. This was another project with a troubling safety history. They'd had a fire last winter, and the building was such a warren of badly-labeled odd floors and unexpected connectors that the firemen got lost in the middle of a four-alarm fire that stretched from the 4th to the 7th floors. The fire was ruled to have been caused by a construction worker's open-flame space heater.

The site was almost all rebuilt after the fire, but like the site that had suffered from bad press about drunks, they had not learned their lesson. The fire exits were now clearly marked, at least. But it was winter, and I suspected there were still open-flame space heaters hiding on site. Why did I suspect this?

They were allowed to use electric heaters, but not overnight, and those took quite a while to reheat a space–but no one was coming in early enough to heat up their changing rooms before the men came in. Hm. So I did an audit on a Saturday, when almost no one was there. I knew how to find dangerous heaters; they'd be in the trade's "shanties" – the plywood temporary buildings where each of the trades changed clothes, stored tools, and kept their records. And I knew what to look for: just outside the shanty there'd be a camouflaged propane cylinder, like you'd use for your barbecue grill.

I found several of these, by crawling under or climbing behind the shanties. I noted which trade's shanty was illegally heated. I took pictures and shared them with the client, the general contractor. And I let them deal with it. They were grateful and they wrote up the offending subcontractors and directed them to fix it or they would withhold payments. That part of this brief assignment went well.

Another plus was my experiencing the sheer technical beauty of the newly constructed concert hall. The fellow who was in charge of all the wiring and controls showed me how the tech wizards were going to do their magic, behind the scenes, to make concerts come to life. Amazing stuff.

What was really amazing was the lack of records for me to box up at the end of this job. Maybe they got lost in the fire. At any rate, I informed my office that I could not conjure missing records out of thin air, and was getting very tired of cleaning up other safety engineers' messes. Could they please stop sending me into records-keeping hells?

BEANIES, BABY

MY NEXT PROJECT REQUIRED TECHNICAL EXPERTISE. I WAS POSTED FOR A couple of weeks at the Four Seasons Hotel on 57th Street. They were doing some rather dangerous work. But before I tell you the nature of the danger, let me set the scene.

The Four Seasons Hotel is one of the most prestigious—and expensive—hotels in New York City. It's situated on 57th between Park Avenue and Madison Avenue. It's in the same neighborhood as Carnegie Hall and exclusive shopping venues such as Bergdorf Goodman. The hotel was originally built during the Great Depression, and was to be known as The Regent, but that project ran into financial difficulties, so the Four Seasons chain took it over and finished it. The Art Deco structure is 53 stories tall, and was designed by the famous architect I.M. Pei. When I was there I actually met Mr. Pei, who'd been brought out of retirement to have the building finished he way he originally intended, and oh, by the way, to turn the top four floors into a private residence for H. Ty Warner, the Beanie Baby billionaire.

The job did not start out well. I made the horrific mistake of going to the main desk on 57th Street to report instead of using the ~~servants~~ I mean trade entrance on 58th Street. But once I found the contractor and was settled in with a tour, I was able to get to work.

The tour was interesting. Everyone who used an elevator was under the constant scrutiny of multiple cameras, which I guess made sense considering the security concerns of guest who would pay over $700 a night. I took the elevator to the top floors and toured the four-floor living space that was under construction. There was an actual wood-burning fireplace on each of the four floors, and the windows up there had to be incredibly thick to handle the wind and other stresses.

My job was to oversee the hoisting and installation of six-inch-thick window glass sheets being brought up the side of this building. The glass sheets were stabilized by a set of frames so they would not twist in the wind and break against the side of the structure. A master rigger was on hand and he designed the entire apparatus, from one setback roof to another, thus absolving me of any professional liability in the design, if not the execution, of the lift. I did copy down his master rigger's license number, but merely because I was going by the book. I was happy with his set up. The area under the lift was adequately blocked off, with flagging to keep people out. So I examined where the glass came back into the building.

That's where I ran into something interesting. The glass had to go up slowly. The fellow who was waiting to received the hoisted glass at the top had what was mostly a boring job, with a tremendous amount of waiting in between bringing in the loads. The hoisting apparatus would make enough noise that a book or even a radio at low volume would be a good way to pass the time. But no, he'd brought a small telescope.

I was only amused until my friendly, "Hello, see anything interesting?" got the following response:

"No, you only see the good stuff at night."

It was then that I realized he was not looking at boats on the river, or the horizon. His telescope was trained on the windows of a nearby apartment building.

Did I say anything? I debated it, and then chose to ignore it as the weather was bright and sunny and would be for several days. I did, however, say something quietly to the rigger he worked for, and the telescope was gone the next day.

Once the glass was brought into the lowest level of the residence, it was carefully wheeled to places where the contractor had cut precise slits in the concrete that did not harm any utilities between the floors. The heavy glass was then brought up through those slits via a chainfall. You may haves seen a chainfall being used to lift an engine out of a car, but they can be used to lift other heavy things on a construction site. The advantage on this site, which had the power turned off, was that it only required muscles to bring up the glass gradually and safely.

All too soon the glass was up and they were forming concrete to fill in the floor slits. The rigger took down his equipment. Time to move on.

Well, they knew I liked railroad jobs. How about another NYC Transit site? Yes.

WESTCHESTER YARD

JUST OFF THE WHITESTONE BRIDGE WAS ANOTHER JOB THAT NO ONE WANTED to go to, because of the cost of the bridge tolls and the long commute. I just laughed at the distance, in part because I needed the quiet time during the drive. More importantly, though, my philosophy was that if I cheerfully made the boss' life easier I'd not get laid off when times got tough. And times would get tough, eventually.

I'd watched the cyclical nature of construction work since I was a child. Our nextdoor neighbor on one side was a union steamfitter, in heavy construction, and the house on the other side of us belonged to a home improvements contractor. Their fortunes rose and fell with the economy. Then my ex was in construction, and I'd been at least on the edges of that industry ever since. Home remodeling, heavy construction: it was all predicated on funding, and when money got tight, there were layoffs. I cheerfully did what has necessary now against that day.

One upshot of this location was that the Yardmaster helped me get Transit discounted tickets to a Broadway show for one of my sons and his girlfriend. Another was that I finally, finally was told my graduation certificate was ready, a year and a half after turning in my last two courses. The office that had my diploma was right next to the Westchester Yard and I picked it up on a lunch break. I have no words to describe how satisfying that was to hold in my hands.

Other satisfying things were happening. I'd gotten an apartment for myself and my remaining son, Chris. He moved out, and I was almost ready to start dating again. But first, I had moles on my face removed, which left little scars and bandages all over my face.(I told the men that "you should have seen the other guy.") I lost weight and got one of those "Lifestyle Lift" partial face lifts.

I'll never forget the looks on the faces of the transit and contractor representatives when I came into a Job Progress Meeting in Manhattan right after that elective facial surgery, and had covered my resulting black eye with a pirate eye patch. Priceless.

Confessions of a Female Safety Engineer

The Westchester Avenue Yard was another train maintenance facility. There was a large building when the trains were repaired—brakes, interior lighting, and air conditioning, mostly—and section where the train interiors were cleaned. The inspectors all knew me from previous jobs and I could even joke with them. The only problem was that my client was the real joke.

This site was steady work, but for a contractor who wanted to break the safety rules every time I turned my back. I was pretty sure they were fudging on quality, too. It became, at times, an ethical quagmire that I held back by the sheer force of my will.

And I had no idea how disrespectful this crew had been until one day, my boyfriend—I had a boyfriend now—dropped by the site for a visit on his day off.

Sure, they'd given me grudging respect but once they realized I "belonged" to someone who would maybe give them a hard time because I was "his" they were as polite to me as if I were a visiting dignitary. The huge contrast between the sarcastic way I had been barely tolerated before and how careful they were to be polite to me after my boyfriend's visit made me furious. Remember what I said about being an accidental feminist? This incident really drove home the point that they had not respected me because I was female; that they felt men were worthy of respect and I was only tolerated unless I was under a man's "protection."

It was an eye-opener. I now knew what real respect looked like. And I started to insist on it even when I was not associated with some sort of male protector. Any other comments about how irritated this made me might require foul language, and I don't want to lower myself to their level, but...#$&@*!

I followed this annoying client to three more train yards, where they were also removing unreachable hydrants in the middle of rows of electrified tracks. There was one in Greenwood Brooklyn, near the big cemetery, another train yard in the Bronx not too far from the Bronx Zoo, and then they landed the contract to do the same in the largest train yard in the world, the Coney Island Yard.

CONEY ISLAND YARD

CONEY ISLAND YARD HAD DISTANT VIEW OF WHAT WAS LEFT OF THE OLD CONEY Island amusement park and the haze of the ocean to its south. The neighborhood had the NYC Aquarium, and a very Russian immigrant area, Brighton Beach.

This immense yard replaced train wheels, a real specialty. To do that the train barn had scores of overhead horizontal cranes to take the train bodies on and off the flatcars. It also had a paint shop, a welding shop, machinists, a fiberglass shop for the seats, a Plexiglas window shop, plus the usual areas to fix the brakes or the air conditioning. The outside yard was over a mile long on its north/south axis, dipping under Belt Parkway, and nearly three-quarters of a mile wide on an east/west axis. It was immense.

My office was in a weird little guardhouse at the entrance, which I shared with their security. Not that they needed much security. The Metropolitan Transit Authority used to have its own police force, all of whom had been folded into the NYPD in a budgetary move. The NYPD still used the old MTA police firing range just inside the entrance Coney Island Yard. So the place was crawling with cops at all hours. Lots of parking. It was a nice neighborhood with good cheap food within walking distance. It was a long commute for me, but I passed through Jamaica Bay National Park , so it was soothing. If traffic got too bad I took a very southerly route along the barrier beaches, past Coney Island, Long Beach, and Jones Beach, then turned north at the crossroads to Fire Island Beach. My four-cylinder stick shift car hardly used any gas at all, so it was no trouble.

Since I never knew where I would be assigned next, and I had times where all I was paid to do was be on call or wait, I needed my email and mobile internet to work. So years ago, instead of using the boss' annoying MacBook and hoping and praying the client had internet access, I opted to bring in my own laptop with a wireless USB connection from my cell phone company. It was an aging Dell laptop and had served me well, but this was the site where it finally died. Luckily, it was on and extended warranty. Getting it fixed was a nightmare, though.

Confessions of a Female Safety Engineer

The repair man came to my office, but he broke the laptop, twice. Each time he left it in worse shape, until I asked for the last part he broke to be overnighted to me so I could put it in myself. The overnighted part took eight days to get there since the idiot tech who'd broken my computer worse, twice, wrote down the wrong address. I asked Dell for a different warranty tech, and they sent someone from another company. They'd hired the same inept tech, though. At least this time he finally fixed it without breaking anything else.

While my computer was down I used someone else's machine, the Yardmaster's. I ended up friends with the Coney Island Yard's general manager, an incredibly sharp young man who always wore a white lab coat indoors, who later became the head of the whole MTA. We met when I was looking for a rest room I was allowed to use in the huge facility; most required a key and I had no key. He showed me where he hung the key to the executive washroom and encouraged me to use it when I was working near his office. I discovered his predilection for cool bits of engineering and brought him in articles from construction magazines and Wired. Remember, I knew it was all about the relationships. This friendship would come in handy later.

One day, the water pressure went to almost nothing in one of their processes that required water. The yard's General Manager cheerfully informed me he knew that it had to be the fault of one of my crews, excavating. I knew exactly where the pipes were in the road, and where we were working, and boldly bet him breakfast in the employee cafeteria that he was wrong and it was not our fault. We shook on it. He and I both did investigations into the water pressure and I was right, he was wrong. He made a big deal out of very publically paying my debt in front of a lot of people, including some of my crew.

Why do I bring this up? It was only five dollars you say? No, it was a public raising of my status in that I had bested the big boss, and a confirmation of his status when he paid his debt. Such gestures have power in an all-male environment. I had passed a milestone with him when he even agreed to a good-natured bet with me. But remember, I proposed the bet. You have to be very sure that it will be accepted before you try to have a friendly wager with a leader of a male crew, but if you're a woman in such an environment, and you're allowed, I recommend you do it. And if you lose that bet, lose graciously and pay your debt with panache. It's not so much that you become "one of the guys" as it is that you've proved to them that you understand the rules. That goes a long way toward them treating you like a team member.

And when you win, that breakfast can taste like victory.

⚠

I was hardly all fun and games on this site, though. One of the most egregious attempts for Transit to charge a client of mine for overdue maintenance and claim it was construction damage happened immediately after that. I was still in the habit of taking digital job progress photos of the before, during and after conditions in our work area. This time, it caught some Transit workers engaged in actual vandalism to try and get us to pay for some repairs.

It happened this way. There was a water line going half a mile from the middle of the site to a remote shed almost at the southern edge of the yard. This line was exposed and in danger of freezing in the winter. The insulation on it was as ragged as cobwebs, and in desperate need of replacement. I'd already taken photos of it since it was right next to our work area. I caught a crew of three transit workers removing that tattered insulation at a brisk clip. They ignored me.

I took a photo of them, rolled down the window of my car, and waved to them cheerfully. "Hey guys! Are you planning on blaming my client for destroying that insulation?"

The work stopped, and they looked at me and each other warily.

I held up the camera. "I've taken pictures of this area every day since we started working near it, and you're the stars of the one I just took. If you try to charge my client for 'damaging' (I made air quotes with my hands) that insulation, you'll lose. Nice try, though." I wasn't bluffing, and they could tell.

That was exactly what they'd been doing. Their shoulders slumped, and although they resumed taking the insulation down they did it much more slowly, resigned to paying for it themselves. Whatever lesser light had ordered them to do this would not be pleased, but I'd saved my client thousands of dollars in fraudulent costs.

Sometimes the entertainment took different forms. There was that time when an impatient driver refused to listen to our flagperson and drove his car into the newly smoothed but quite wet concrete, for example. The flagperson and I laughed and laughed. I should tell you about her.

One of my coworkers on that particular site was a woman union flagger who was a local resident, pressed upon us by the neighborhood. I'd run into these neighborhood committees at the SCA project in Brownsville, and my instructions from my bosses were to stay completely out of the negotiations, which could be intimidating and nasty. Let the unions and community organizers work with site management to create a few extra jobs in their local area; it was not a safety concern. But this lovely young woman, we'll call her Shahnae, was my responsibility, safety wise. She was a fast learner with a great attitude and I wanted to mentor her while I was there. So when she confessed that her feet were freezing and she the cash to buy some insulated construction boots online but had no credit card, I was happy to help her. I took her money and ordered her boots online. Cabela's saw the Brooklyn address and called me to make sure the charge was authorized, which was appreciated. I had them send it as they would a gift, so there were no identifiers and my card was safe.

Shahnae returned the favor by being the best flagger I ever worked with.

But some of the men on that site were, to put it mildly, out of their league. The worst one was a Transit employee assigned to watch us, a clueless "quality engineer" who could not read blueprints, and was blind to quality issues going on right in front of his nose. He followed us around like a useless shadow, always getting in the way. When he found out I was dating again I heard more than I wanted to know about his abortive sex life. Although he never hit on me the man was so oblivious I was in despair. He put me out of his misery for months by walking backwards into a shallow excavation and injuring himself.

The contractor's supervisors actually laughed when he got hurt, but not the crew. They were all Portuguese. Most of them spoke English very well, too, and although the laborers were hard workers and wonderful fellows, their bosses were another story. Their superintendent longed for the good old days, "... when the Mafia ran construction and you knew what you were up against." Their foreman was the worst corner-cutter on safety and quality issues I had ever met in my life. By the end of our last job together I knew their tricks and had finally showed them that doing it the right way was cheaper, but by then their project manager and the president of the company had made the newspapers by being taken out of their offices in handcuffs, accused of fraud.

But the handcuffs happened years down the road. For now I was stuck on a site with some of the most professional transit engineers (with one "quality engineer" exception) I'd met, and some of the most unprofessional construction guys I'd ever worked with.

On my last week at this job the Transit Authority hosted a Transit "rodeo," an open house for the workers' families and a chance to test their skills at various work-related tasks, with points for speed and accuracy. Antique rail cars were brought in from a museum, and there was a huge catered cookout and live music. I was the only person from our crew invited by the yard's general manager and was allowed to bring a date, who got to fire guns with me in the NYPD indoor shooting range. It was a fitting bit of closure, as that was the last full-time Transit job I was to be on for quite a while.

TIMES SQUARE GETS A FINGER

MY NEW ASSIGNMENT WAS LOCATED JUST ABOVE THE TIMES SQUARE SUBWAY station and a fairly easy job to reach via mass transit. So I called my car insurance company and asked for the much cheaper rate that covered me only driving to and from the local commuter rail, and bought a monthly ticket to NYC for the Long Island Railroad and a monthly subway Metrocard. The cost of these monthly tickets was about the same as the cost of driving into NYC which was astronomical in not only insurance but gasoline and wear and tear. My commute, either way, still came to about $400 a month. It got a little more expensive when I had to buy weekly or individual LIRR tickets, but that was rare.

Ah, Times Square. The Theater District. To be that close to the heart of NYC and be too busy to visit any of it! Tourists swirled around me outside this venue, humanity so thick on the sidewalks that pedestrians spilled over into streets that cars had trouble driving through. Subway cars shrieked to a stop beneath it, and a visual cacophony of competing advertisements and lighting shrieked above it.

Times Square is the throbbing heart of New York City

My construction project was renovation of the headquarters for Thompson Reuters. The rooms had deep floors full of computer cables a foot under the removable tiles. When I joined the job it was nearly done. I was there a few months while Reuters was moving in, floor by floor, and during the time when the level just above the sidewalk was vacated by the trades and slowly turned into one store after another of a new retail mall. They were also finishing things on the roof, and I was often up there drinking my morning coffee while enjoying a windswept dawn with a phenomenal view from 53 stories above the world. I could see the Hudson River and NJ to the west, Central Park to the north, and the East River and Brooklyn to the east. They should have charged admission for that view, really. I'd work my way down walking daily through the construction spaces, noting problems and getting them fixed.

167

Confessions of a Female Safety Engineer

I was there on a weekend when they put the sign on the building with a crane. Another building, down 42nd Street, was getting a sign that day, too. It's not often you see a giant plastic finger taking up an entire flatbed semi, but they were delivering part of the sculpture going on the roof signage at the new *Madame Tussauds Wax Museum* a block over. Only in New York, people.

I walked past Madame Tussauds and saw some wax figures of famous people they occasionally put on the sidewalk to draw in customers. I never had time to go in, though, nor could I afford it.

A larger concern to me were things I could see hanging off the building across 42nd Street. Steel erectors were not following fall protection procedures on an adjacent project. It was not my site, but I quietly mentioned what I'd seen to someone I knew over there. The fall protection situation over there seemed to improve, for a while. But then I was very sad when they lost a couple of workers to fatal falls. Things looked much safer across the street after the deaths, but closing the proverbial barn doors after the horse is gone would do nothing for the lost men, or for their loved ones. I noted the name of this contractor and the ironworking sub in question. They are both out of business, now.

I also did overtime on part of the Times Square subways station rehabilitation after my full day at Thompson Reuters. Sometimes I had time for a reasonably priced dinner between the projects at BB Kings. If I did overtime, I could expense that.

But once the project was over, I was moved again. This time, I went from Times Square to Fifth Avenue.

HYATT ON LIBRARY ROW

THIS WAS ANOTHER JOB I COULD TAKE MASS TRANSIT TO, AND I'D DONE NIGHT work on the subway station across the street from my new project, so the white-on-white polar bears cut out in tile were a familiar sight and conjured memories of bringing top-heavy equipment safely down hidden stairs.

The new job was right across from the main branch of the New York Public Library, which I had never visited, and a bunch of shops on 41st Street known as Library Row. Later, I was able to meet with friends at the immense library, and went inside it for the first time. It was gorgeous, a real architectural treasure. But first, let me tell you about the new job.

My latest project was going to be a hotel on two lots. One lot was on Fifth Avenue across from the Library, with its famous stone lion guardians, Patience and Fortitude. Well, the hotel *rooms* were over Fifth Avenue, but the actual entrance was going to be on West 40th Street so they could rent out retail space on Fifth. During construction, that's where our office was, in what would become a Fifth Avenue storefront.

The other property that was going to be part of the hotel was on West 41st Street, on Library Row. The two properties were to be connected with an atrium impressive enough to be worthy of an upscale hotel in New York's Manhattan, on Fifth Avenue. I'd seen the plans. But for now, it was a recently stopped job in serious, serious trouble. Remember when I said demolition companies doing renovations were in the bad habit of destroying things that should remain? In this case, they'd demolished something that was needed, critical to the ongoing fire protection of a building under construction.

Let me tell you a few pertinent facts about fire protection on a high rise construction site. As you build up from the ground, when you get to a certain floor, you have to have a "dry standpipe." This pipe typically runs up fire escape stairs and is a way for the fire department to pump water up to either sprinklers or at least places on each floor that firemen can attach their hoses. When you do top-down, full demolition, the dry standpipe can only be demolished to two floors below your highest floor. You've probably seen that big standpipe connector capped in the sidewalk area for the firemen to attach the standpipe to a hydrant or pumper. On a construction site this standpipe connector has signage, and it is marked with a red light so that firefighters can find it quickly.

This same standpipe will also be part of the permanent fire protection for a building. At that point it is usually attached to a water tank on the roof that lets the initial burst of water come down through the sprinklers at the first hint of a fire in what is now a "wet standpipe."

To make intact standpipes even more important, there had recently been a horrible fire at the Deustche Bank building across from the World Trade Center. This structure was damaged on 9/11 and was finally being demolished. The Fire Department had given permission for the demolition contractor to take one of the two standpipes out. During demolition there was a fire was on the 17th floor, and FDNY assumed that the other, legally-required standpipe was intact. But some of the demolition guys had cut holes in the one remaining standpipe on two floors, so that they could feed oxygen and acetylene hoses up through it.

When the Deustche Bank fire happened, some firemen attached a nearby hydrant to the standpipe, while others raced up to the fire floor and...nothing came out of the damaged standpipe. Two firefighters died, and 100 more had almost died in a maze of asbestos removal areas cordoned off from the rest of the building. Only their fire axes had saved them.

So let's just say that FDNY was on the warpath about illegally demolishing standpipes at the moment. And my job had recently cut out both standpipes, *and* demolished both fire stairs, on the 40th street side.

FDNY and the building department had stopped the job. Stopping the job was expensive. There were conditions to restarting the job. The interim measures FDNY insisted on until a new standpipe was installed were expensive, too. The fire department had required the entire building to be surrounded with a scaffold with two scaffold stairways that were wide enough to handle a fireman in full kit, at the contractor's expense. And they insisted on a sort of freestanding standpipe that had hose connections on each floor, even though it was not in a stairway.

What was absolutely fascinating is that nobody told me about this site's recent history. I was just thrown on the site by my boss, who assumed the client would tell me what had happened. The client assumed that my company had explained the situation. I had to figure it out for myself. I came back after my first walk-through and asked the client about the free-floating standpipe with an incredulous, *What the hell is that?*

Needless to say, getting some fire stairs with at least one working standpipe was a top priority. Until we had proper stairs and proper standpipe(s), a fire in this building would be awkward. So I made very sure that all the fire extinguishers that should be deployed were deployed in their proper positions, and that all hot work had permits and firewatchers. I paid special attention to housekeeping, especially when it impacted a clear means of egress or if it involved piles of combustible materials.

There were other issues, too. On the 41st Street side of the project, they were doing demolition above adjacent buildings. There was a perfectly acceptable demolition plan, that allowed for any hazards to the adjacent buildings to be stopped by providing plank and foam protection on the roof of those structures. There was only one problem; one of the adjacent buildings—a cigar shop— would not allow them on their roof to protect it.

On my fifth day there, with me barely filled in on site history, we had a visit by the absolute head of the FDNY, the late Fire Commissioner Nicholas Scoppetta. A very powerful man. He could close their job again if things were not handled exactly the way he wanted. I cannot tell you how nervous my client was! And I, despite the client's panicked looks and gestures that I should be silent as they walked the site with the Commissioner and me, decided that I would treat him like any inspector I wanted to befriend.

This was the man who had been in charge of the FDNY on 9/11. He must have all *sorts* of instructive stories to tell. So I treated him like another human being, and asked him all about his command. I told him I'd bet he had all kinds of fascinating experiences in that organization. He smiled, and agreed, and told me—us—about times he'd seen this and that violation or thing done correctly. He seemed glad that anyone wanted to ask him, and went into instructor mode. I did not have to feign my awe at the fact that such an important man was interested in teaching us. I was sincerely grateful and paying attention. I was listening, and not because of what he was, but who he was as a person.

Confessions of a Female Safety Engineer

He looked at our scaffold stairs for his men, the temporary standpipe, and the new stairs being built and while he was not thrilled with conditions they were acceptable because of the obvious fire-safety mentality on the site. His only question was when would the new fire stairs and standpipes be available for his men? My client was able to give him definitive dates and they parted on courteous terms.

"I just about had a heart attack when you started talking to that guy," the project manager admitted, "but you handled the Commissioner exactly right."

I was transferred out right after the first fire stair and standpipe were finished, and they'd taken down the scaffolding with its fire stairs.

The cigar shop must have been finally mollified somehow, for the hotel was eventually built. Oh, and I think my old construction office there is a Sunglass Hut now.

But I'd been transferred to the very job that the disgraced safety manager went to, the one who'd let the fire stairs and standpipes be recklessly demolished. I wondered, not kindly, what sort of mess she'd left for me at her next site.

THE BOOB JOB

ABOUT THIS TIME I MOVED TO A NEW APARTMENT ON LONG ISLAND'S NORTH shore since my last son, Chris, had moved out and gotten married. I was sent to a project I'd been on for a weekend crane stint: the Memorial Sloan Kettering Breast and Imaging Center, usually abbreviated as MSKBIC. The men were concerned I'd be offended so I was on the site for a year and a half before one of them shamefacedly admitted that their nickname for it was "the Boob Job." Made sense to me.

I was proud to be a part of it. The 17-story building was going to be a breast cancer center that, when completed, would have everything from X-rays and MRI facilities, to outpatient chemo rooms, to a mastectomy boutique that would have breast forms and all sorts of fashionable ways to get on with your life when you were a breast cancer survivor. Awesome stuff.

I'd been requested by the project manager, Scott, as I'd hit it off with him during some weekend crane work. As was my custom, I'd gotten there early that Saturday. The crane had started lifting things before they were allowed to by their permits, and I'd shut them down before the project manager even arrived. My competence and attitude impressed him favorably, the existing safety manager was not doing a good job (she was the one who'd allowed both standpipes to be removed in the hotel across from the NY Public Library!), and boom. I was in.

It's hard to encapsulate everything that went on in my nearly two years there, so as usual I will share the interesting stories, the vignettes. But before I do I want to say that this was the most professional and safety-minded management team that I ever worked with. Turner Construction did not have to be told that safety, done right, saves you money; they lived and breathed it. As a rule, I'd found that the closer you got to the top construction companies in the world, the safer they were – and Turner was one of the top ten. Everyone there was totally professional, top-to-bottom, and it was a privilege to be a part of that team.

Confessions of a Female Safety Engineer

There were some annoyances, like the fact that there was no way to get there via mass transit that did not take over three hours each way, so I had to drive and pay the $14 per day workman's rate to park. And overall it was too-nice a neighborhood, $3 to even get a cup of coffee. But my policy was not to gripe to Consulting Inc. about my postings. There *would* be an economic downturn, eventually, and I continued to intentionally generate good will so that I would not be laid off in the ensuing downturn.

I was introduced to the site labor foreman, Lou, and the flamboyant project superintendent, Willie. Willie was a pudgy man who wore purple suits, a black shirt and tie, and had a haircut like a rock star, which were outrageous affectations in such a dusty and macho environment and would not have been tolerated unless he was very good indeed. My desk was in a group office that I shared with a mechanical engineer, three junior supers, and a friend from the Bellevue job, Michael. They were a great bunch of guys.

As was my custom, on my first full day on the site I asked for a phone contact list, not just because I needed to reach people to fix problems but because my experience told me that if the phone list had not been kept up to date, other things would be lacking. I asked for a copy of their CPM (computerized project management) schedule, for if they were behind schedule they would cut corners on safety and the schedule would show me the most likely places they'd try to shave time by breaking the rules. Both were in order and the job was on schedule, a virtually unheard of situation in my experience. I looked at their injury files to see if they had a pattern of certain injuries to watch out for. Nothing stood out.

Then I looked at the floor plans to map the route of my first inspection. You usually find a set of things that need fixing on a first walk-through, and a good safety engineer always focuses on the hazard most likely to kill or injure, and then on the ones most likely to freak out an insurance or OSHA inspector, or an inspector from the NYC Department of Buildings (the BEST Squad). As I mentioned, my company's management told me that the previous safety manager had "not been doing a good job," so I wanted to see what they meant by that.

My 17-floor inspection found one major issue that had to be fixed right away. The temporary construction lighting, those bulbs in yellow cages that run through an area you're building, were not being maintained. It was some of the worst lighting I'd ever seen, with hundreds of burnt out bulbs and ceiling wires sagging to the floors in places. I was appalled. And it was the responsibility of my old nemesis, the Local 3 electricians.

Well, there were ways around their recalcitrance.

I asked Willie the Turner super if I could set up a meet with the site electrical superintendent and that Willie stay with me as a witness as I spoke to him. Willie said he needed a smoke break and he'd set it up out in front of the main entrance in fifteen minutes. He introduced me to the head electrician on the site, we'll call him Frank. And here is pretty much how *that* conversation went.

Me: Frank, we have a problem with the temporary lighting on site. There are lots of dark areas and burnt out bulbs.
Frank: We have a man who maintains the temp lighting, full time.
Me: I had no idea they let guide dogs onto construction sites.

Frank, bristling, gave me a very long speech about how it was not the electricians' fault. Central to his theme was that the other trades broke the bulbs and they could not keep up with it. I heard this injustice described in about ten different ways.

Standard communications protocol says you repeat back to the person what they've said, but in different words, so they know you've really heard them. So I did that.

Frank elaborated on even more ways it was not the electricians' fault that the lighting was in such bad shape. I repeated them back to him, too.

All the while, Willie just stood there in his purple suit and black tie, smoking, not saying a word. I could tell he knew what I was up to, and silently approved. We patiently gave the fellow time to spin more rope to hang himself.

After about the third time I repeated the gist of the head electrician's arguments, I asked if he was done. Frank piously sputtered on with a few more self-justifications. I asked again, "Are you done, is it my turn?" A few more self-serving excuses trickled out, and I noted them back to him, not judging the rightness or wrongness of his statements, not out loud.

Finally, Frank said he was done. And then, whenever he tried to break into the conversation, Willie patiently reminded him that he'd said he was done, and it was my turn. I laid out the situation as I saw it. I requested help bringing the building up to the construction lighting standards, citing OSHA regulations about minimum foot-candles and such.

Frank the electrician super informed me that he would be more than happy to fix any problems; I just had to tell him where they were.

Now knowing where the lighting problems were located was *his* problem, and Frank was trying to offload it onto me. But that was just what I hoped he'd say. I agreed to do that and we parted politely.

By the end of the day I had a two-page, 10-point font spreadsheet that a listed locations of all of the site's burnt-out bulbs, missing yellow lighting cages, crushed sockets, drooping lighting wires, and missing lighting for all 17 floors, plus the basement. It came to over 50 lines per page, with multiple items on most lines. But why hand *that* to Frank?

I walked over the project manager Scott's office, and asked him if it would be acceptable to send the spreadsheet and a nice note to Frank's *boss*. You have to ask the client for permission to pull a stunt like that; sometimes it's not the right time, like when they are negotiating a big change order. But Scott's grin split his face as he reached for his rolodex to give me that email addy. Scott asked for a copy of it as a blind cc. I charitably decided to cc Frank on it, too.

The next morning a contrite Frank came into my office, hat literally in hand, and informed me politely that it was "not necessary" to send such things to his boss. I could give them to him directly.

I replied, barely looking up from my paperwork, that I supposed that would depend on how the lighting was maintained from now on. And dismissed him with a polite thank you.

For some funny reason, we never had a problem with the temporary lighting on that site, ever again.

⚠️

Another obsessive, floor-by-floor inspection saved our bacon on that site. This time, the issue was fire safety: specifically, smoking inside jobsites. The fire department, FDNY, had teamed up with the NYC Department of Buildings on a fine schedule that either of them could inspect and cite you with. It was a fine per cigarette butt.

The only way I could think to enforce it was to do an obsessive-compulsive micro inspection of the entire building, looking for cigarette butts and picking them *all* up.

I know, ew. I wore gloves.

It took three days to make the building butt-free, with the enthusiastic assistance of a new "fire watch" security guard who happened to be walking through the building at the same time I was. I carefully saved the nasty box of butts in case I needed to drag it out at a job progress meeting to prove that we actually had a problem with workers smoking on the site. Despite the butts being sealed in a plastic bag, my desk smelled like an ashtray until I got rid of the things.

The main place I'd found the butts was in the stairwells or roof spaces, the usual places men went for a quick smoke and the first places FDNY or the BEST Squad would look. The other place I found most of the butts was behind the Local 3 electricians' shanty. I had a private meeting with Frank , and told him to please have his men take their smoke breaks outside. I told him I had personally picked up every single #&%@ butt in this building and would know if they were generating more. After the way I'd pushed him to maintain the temporary lighting, he resented it but complied. He believed I'd follow through.

The subcontractors got the message when Turner's project manager, Scott, laid the law down at a job meeting.

Now that I knew the building was clear of old butts, I was able to track who had been working in any areas where we found any new cigarette butts. We wrote them up and fined them. FDNY found a couple of butts, and fined us. Thanks to my hard work, we could pass those fines on to the guilty parties. After that happened a couple of times, the violations stopped and I could get rid of my cache of old butts and spray the inside of my desk with Febreeze.

Oh, the glamour.

⚠

Then, there was Frank's revenge.

I was offered (by one of his men, so I should have been suspicious) some free low carb bars, and I took a box, eating two for lunch. They contained lycasin, a sugar substitute, and when anything with that stuff is past its expiration date, well... if you eat it you'll have happen to you what happened to me.

Horrible gas. And emissions so noxious I could not even stand to be in the same room with myself. With no way to stop it until it worked its way out of my system, which took 48 hours.

Willie's labor foreman, Lou, who had risen as a team through the organization with Willie, caught one of the worst of these emissions. His good-natured teasing about me having gas went on for days. At about this time, for no reason, I suddenly realized that the flamboyant superintendent Willie and I had the same long, layered haircut. When I shared this observation with my friend Michael, he assumed I would mention it to Willie right away. "No, I think I will save that observation for some other time, when it might be of use."

Michael was surprised, but I knew that such zingers were much more effective if you waited for an opportune moment to use them.

A couple of days later in the afternoon Willie came into our group office, as he often did, to go over the schedule for the next day. When he was done, as an afterthought he turned to me, grinned and said, "So, Wendy. I understand you have a problem with gas."

I just looked at Michael.

No, his return look said, *you're not going to use that now...are you? Oh crap, you're gonna say it!*

With exactly the same inflection to my voice, I deadpanned, "So Willie. I understand you and I have the same haircut."

He turned beet red as he ran his hand through his hair and realized as he said it, "Yeah. Yeah I guess I do." And he beat a hasty retreat. I swear, the guys all tried to not laugh until he was out of earshot.

They failed, miserably, but they at least tried. For a millisecond. Maybe.

And the next day Willie came in with a much shorter haircut. No one, absolutely no one in my group office mentioned it. We did not even start grinning madly at each other or shaking our heads and snorting until he left the room.

Wendy S. Delmater

As well as I got along with Willie, and I really did, there was one time where I had to set my posture with him.

Here was the situation that day. I was limping with what would eventually be diagnosed as a large benign tumor embedded in my thigh muscle, but Willie had an emergency, so he asked me to help flag in a stone delivery. The huge flatbed delivery semi would not fit in the area the stone needed to be stored, so he found a place where the truck could idle, not actually park, but remain "standing" while forklifts unloaded it. The only problem was that the forklifts had to be flagged across the intersection of E. 66th Street and busy 2nd Avenue. It would take two flagmen and he was short a man. Could I help?

Sure, I'd flagged before. I did not mention my physical discomfort, but put off my inspection of the rest of the building, and my paperwork, and went out there and flagged for almost four hours. I had a ten minute lunch break where I hit the rest room and grabbed a sandwich, and went right back out there. Then I walked the rest of the building and started on my paperwork.

I've not touched on the paperwork aspects of being a safety manager, but I handled: a daily Site Safety Manager's log, daily close out open items on old SSM logs, coordinating safety training for 50 subcontractors, individual and new subcontractor orientations, report follow-ups from the insurance company, hot work permits, monthly reports, crane preplanning, and more.

And for some reason Willie came in, in front of the rest of the guys in my group office, and proceeded to dress me down. He said I "spent too much time in the office." He yelled that my work was out there, not just sitting in here all the time. He growled insinuations that I was lazy and not doing my job. The younger men I shared my office with held their breaths. You could hear a pin drop.

My first instinct, as a woman, was to placate, smooth things, try to reason with him, or put up with it. But then, I intentionally set that instinct aside. Instead, I asked myself a serious question, *How would a man handle this?* I knew how a guy would answer him, knew that his claims were baseless. And, frankly I did not need this project.

I faced Willie more calmly than I felt, still seated in my swivel chair, facing him, not my desk. "Willie, despite you pulling me off my work to flag for you for four hours, and me only getting a 10-minute lunch break—the other guys in the office can testify to that—I still managed to walk the entire building and I am writing my report. There is a lot more paperwork to this job than you realize. But, fine. If you're not happy with my work ask my company to send you someone else. I have three other projects clamoring for me to work for them, at the moment." In other words, *I'm sorry you feel that way but you're wrong, and I don't need you.* Then, in a crowning insult, I turned my back on him and swiveled my chair back to my desk. "Now if you'll excuse me, I have some paperwork to do," I added. There was an audible intake of breath from the other engineers in the room. I could hear Willie breathing heavily, absolutely furious. I ignored him as my heart pounded, and went back to work.

If you're going to push back like that you have to be absolutely certain you do not need the other person. I was. I was also secure in the fact that his boss, the project manager, wanted me there and would probably have me stay. If things were strained between me and Willie after that, it would be his fault, not mine. It was no longer up to me.

The next day, Willie came in when none of the other men were in the office, and apologized to me. He said he has not been feeling well the other day and he had been off base. I told him to think nothing of it; we all have off days, and we worked cordially together until the end of the project.

The younger engineers in my group office sort of tiptoed around me in awe for a week until their shock wore off. *Nobody* told Willie off, and yet I just had, and yet Willie and I were still friendly with each other. Willie screamed a lot, but I knew it was usually a tactic to get what he wanted. In the military this is literally called "being pissed off for show." So usually, Willie yelling was nothing personal, just business.

However, this time Willie made baseless, inaccurate accusations about my work on a day when I had gone far out of my way to help him. That was not like him.

"I was not feeling well" is a one-size-fits-all excuse and will cover a multitude of sins if it's used sparingly. Everyone has bad days. I have no idea if Willie's best friend died or someone keyed his car to set him off but when a person ranges that far outside of their normal behavior patterns, it helps to think it's probably not *you* they were upset with. If the working relationship is to be salvaged, just accept the lame apology and pretend it never happened. That's what I did, but only after I refused to accept unwarranted accusations. Willie and I worked together as well as ever after his outburst and apology.

But the young men in the office with me treated me differently after I stood up to Willie, and while I supposed that was part of being management, part of me wanted to restore our easy camaraderie and not be so admired. Since they often rummaged in my desk to borrow a pen, and I was rarely in the office, what I planned to do was to leave something for them to find. I wanted to have a fancy empty box made, engraved with the words "Big Brass Ones" and a sign inside that said, "If box is empty, item is in use."

But I never got around to it. As usual, I was simply too busy for the finer things in life.

Left Hanging

I'VE NOT TALKED MUCH ABOUT THE WORK I HAD TO DO CHECKING HANGING scaffolds, but if there was any such of scaffold on the job it was part of my duties to oversee its safe installation, operation, and dismantling. The MSKBIC project had a hanging scaffold, used to finish the installation of the windows from the outside. I was supposed to check any such scaffold's PE drawings when it came in, and its anchor points and the separate tie points for the workers on it, daily, on which ever roof it was tied to. Then I was supposed to check the scaffold itself: nothing stacked above the railings? Debris netting on the guardrail in place? Were the men tied off, and tied off properly?

The building was a wedding-cake design, with smaller and smaller sections on top that had little adjacent roof areas. The long metal scaffold was heavy, motorized, and was usually parked on one of those smaller roof sections when not in use.

One morning the men went to work on this scaffold, and its motors were gone. They had not used the scaffold since last Thursday, and it was Tuesday. The motors were quite expensive, worth over $3,000 each. This was a major theft.

We called in the NYPD to report the theft and a detective came to investigate. When the contractor called to rent two new motors from their supplier, the supplier told them that someone had tried to sell them two motors on Saturday. Their rep had feigned interest and gotten parts of the serial numbers, which matched our missing ones. The scaffold rep told the seller he'd have to ask how much he could pay for them, and the seller left a phone number. Our team checked it against people who worked here, and it belonged to an elderly laborer, six months from retirement, who'd been very vocal about the security guards getting fire watch training and taking away what he considered *his* overtime. Further, the scaffolding company had CCTV footage of the man trying to sell the motor. It was him, all right. The police quickly got a warrant and found the scaffold motors in a utility shed on his property.

Confessions of a Female Safety Engineer

It was a very sad business, quickly concluded. I felt the sorriest for the laborer's brother, a foreman also on the site, who went under suspicion as an accessory and was suspended until the mess was cleared up. The whole thing was just so very sad and unnecessary.

⚠

Sad things happened on jobsites, from time to time. Two blocks away, an anchor point strap embedded in the concrete and wrapped around a steel beam gave way, and a very young man was plunged to his death. Word went out throughout the city that all such anchor points should be checked. As a follow up, all of the site safety managers working for Turner were instructed to audit all of the slings and lanyards on our sites. I spent an entire day doing so—you can imagine how careful I was to check them all after checking for cigarette butts and burnt out bulbs—and I sent the resulting report to the assistant safety director in charge of my job and four others. We'll call him Malik.

Now sometimes the internet eats your email, and this was one of those few times. Although I had my inventory notes, I'd put the report directly into the email, and it somehow disappeared. Malik got in trouble because of my missing report and steadfastly refused to believe I had ever sent it. He was convinced I was a liar, he was furious that I'd made him look bad, and he did every vindictive thing he could think of from that point on to make my life miserable and pay me back for embarrassing him.

One fine weekend, Memorial Sloan Kettering, the Owner (construction-speak for the entity we were building this project for) wanted help with something. The Owner was bringing in two massive electro-superconducting magnets for their MRI units, and wanted to Turner to be there to for expert assistance with this potentially hazardous work. It was not in Turner's contract, but they said they'd be there. I was asked to be there, too.

It was very involved, the sort of non-routine situation that safety managers do meticulous safety planning for in advance. I did the pre-planning. There were going to be a warren of street and sidewalk closure permits to see to, crane permits and exclusion zones, and the magnets themselves on a flatbed truck, still steaming from their bath in some super-cold liquid. The magnets were not magnetized unless current went through them so at least that would not be an issue.

The huge magnets were to be lowered via the crane through openings that had been intentionally cut through the roof of the Faraday cages we'd carefully built around the MRI rooms. These square reinforced ceiling sections had lift points for the crane to pull them out, using massive embedded eyebolts. There were steel double-door roof hatches above that. One of the delivery crew was to tie off onto a nice, safe anchor point that was part of the permanently installed window washing track. He would attach the crane's four-point sling to the ceiling section's lift points, and guide the crane as it took out the ceiling sections, and as they lowered in the magnets. The crane loads would all have guide ropes on them, to control them. Two men were going to be positioned in the MRI rooms to bolt the magnets onto their frames.

So the preplanning was done, and the required pre-job safety briefing delivered and signed for by all involved. Everyone knew what to expect. The crane operator was set up and his credentials checked out. The DOT permits were being followed, an exclusion zone was around the crane's swing area and a flagman was there to keep pedestrians out. I photographed that everything was set up and had copies of all the relevant training accomplished and the permits on my clipboard.

In all the time I had been on this site, the roof hatches above those MRI rooms had never been opened. As the man to attach the lift points was tying off, I peered into the first open roof hatch, and saw nothing amiss. The ceiling section we were lifting out had raw plywood on top, with a frame done in two-by-fours where they'd cut through the MRI room ceiling and its Faraday cage, and arrows to match everything up into its former orientation when they replaced the ceiling section. There were huge eyebolts to lift the section out. The man who was going to hook the crane's rigging to the anchor points hopped in to connect the crane's four-point sling to it.

What we did not know about was the man-sized hole that someone had cut through the ceiling section for access and plugged back in. It was perfectly camouflaged, with every the grain of the wood matching. The man who was to attach the crane sling to the ceiling lift points put his weight on this camouflaged opening and fell right in. But since he was tied off, he only scraped his side and his ribs and did not fall14 feet to the MRI room floor.

Still, he needed medical attention. And when you call an ambulance to a construction site, you also get NYC building inspectors, who are ready to find fault with *everything*.

I was deep into making an analysis of what had gone wrong and making an incident report while being a first responder to the man who was injured, taking photos of what happened, keeping witnesses separate to get untainted reports, dealing with letting the building department know, my consulting boss know, and the client's safety department know.

The last thing I needed was Malik, crawling all over the accident site, getting in the way while trying to use this incident to harm me professionally. But there he was, with blood in his eye, being a distraction and a nuisance.

Sadly, I was not the least bit surprised when I got a furious call from the Turner's NY District Safety manager, we'll call him Hitch, who'd believed all of Malik's accusations. I replied with equal heat that Malik had had it in for me since the missing lanyards report, and NO, I had not left an unprotected "floor hole" if that's what he reported. In fact, the building department had just been here and said it was the best run site they had ever seen and they were not going to fine us! Now would he please excuse me? I had interviews to perform.

Malik was reprimanded and transferred away from me. And soon after that, Hitch offered me a dream job, with Turner. But there was one more project I did for Turner while that was in negotiations.

SOLOW, YOU CAN'T GET UNDER IT

THE NEW PROJECT WAS CALLED SOLOW TOWERS. IT WAS GOING TO BE THE twin of a posh new residential tower near the 59th Street Bridge. Our office was in one of the residential units in the twin building's penthouse, a finished apartment that was carefully covered in kraft paper and plastic. The space had amazing views of the East River, Roosevelt Inland, Queens and Brooklyn.

But the job was downstairs and outside in late Autumn weather. The client was just starting that second, matching residential tower. I came in when they were almost finished excavating the partially-finished foundation and building the beginnings of a parking garage. There was a lot of concrete to be poured, with a lot of rebar tied inside it, and there were column footings to excavate and pour. The excavation had already been carefully shored up so it would not collapse the adjacent streets with expertly engineered steel whalers, a series of braces that kept what would be the multi-level parking garage walls vertical.

One of the subcontractors cut a whaler because it was in his way and there was rather a crisis until we had a structural engineer come in and figure out a solution! The adjacent street which could have collapsed, York Avenue, was a busy feeder to the 59th Street Bridge. But the wall held, and the street held firm, due to built-in over engineered tolerances.

Speaking of engineering tolerances, there were all sorts of little challenges, like for an anchor point for some of the work requiring fall protection. An "anchor point" is where you attach a worker's fall protection harness and lanyard. Per OSHA, it has to handle about 5,000-pounds of force to allow for the mass of a worker, times the velocity of his fall, doubled to have an...engineering tolerance. Basically, an anchor point has to be strong enough to hang an SUV from it. We had a bit of work requiring fall protection and no anchor point in sight. So I had them drive over a piece of heavy equipment to the area—an excavator—and used that. The excavator could hold up an SUV, no problem!

A few months after I was transferred to the Solow job, Bernie Madoff was caught and went to jail for one of the biggest pyramid schemes ever perpetrated.

Confessions of a Female Safety Engineer

The Owner for the project lost his shirt because he was heavily invested with Madoff. After a flurry of meetings, it was decided to finish and cap the parking garage, as they could charge for the resulting parking spaces, and finish the foundations in case the residential tower project ever resumed. All around the city, other projects faltered and closed.

This was the beginning of the 2008-2009 crash. The economic downturn that I knew would come to the construction industry, someday, was now here.

Fear was everywhere, as those who wrapped up this job knew that there might not be work for them when it was over. I had to calm tensions from near fist-fight levels at times. One by one, staff was laid off until I was one of the last people there. I'm still using some of the office supplies they gave me when they left the site.

The job offer from Turner evaporated when they started laying their safety managers off. My employer, Consulting Inc., started layoffs as well. But I was not one of the layoffs. Soon the new, smaller scope of the project officially meant it no longer was a "major building," and the project no longer needed a licensed site safety manager. So it was time for a new jobsite.

Target and Shell Game

The next big project I was on was so remote it would have been a four-hour trip each way on mass transit: two hours into Manhattan and then two more on subways. So, I was driving to and from work again, this time on the Belt Parkway to Flatbush Avenue. It was a very long commute, but I at least not in rush hour traffic. I ended up driving when almost no one was on the road due to my extremely long hours.

The job was called Target Triangle. The client was building a two-story department store with a multi-level parking garage on the roof and retail stores at the street level, below. It was poised at the very base of the last subway stop going south on Flatbush Avenue from Manhattan to where it crossed Nostrand Avenue. The general contractor was a firm from Pennsylvania that had never worked in NYC before, and they kept running into the unexpected with the City. The project was therefore behind schedule, but the store absolutely had to open on time or they would be charged *a million dollars a day* in damages. As I've mentioned previously, the minute a job gets behind schedule they are tempted to cut corners on safety. And these folks were motivated to cut corners to a fare-thee-well.

Some of their problems with NYC had been non-trivial, too, so the City was watching the project carefully. For example, there was a freight railroad spur running under the job. Before I arrived there'd been an incident down there. The project had needed to erect something right next to the tracks, so they built a scaffold to do it. But they built that scaffold in the train's right of way. They did not allow for the width of trains coming through, and a moving freight train was damaged while ripping the scaffold out. At least no one had been working on that scaffold. But the railroad, and NYC, were not pleased.

The safety manager I was replacing had no rail experience, so maybe that's why they sent me there even though work in the area near the rails was done. The guy I replaced was a retired BEST Squad construction safety inspector from the Department of Buildings, who'd let the fact that he had his own office

189

and could order supplies go to his head. I had not seen this many unneeded supplies, ordered just because a person *could*, since I'd done weekend work at the now-defunct NYC Department of Education headquarters, where there were 40-yard dumpsters full of school supplies that department heads had ordered so their funding would be used up and they'd get the same amount of money next year. Not donated to charity, school supplies just thrown out. That had made me furious at the waste of tax dollars.

But the insane amount of office supplies in my new office at the Target Triangle project just made me sad. I sent a lot of it to fellow safety managers and my company's main office, especially when the client got rid of the safety trailer and put me in a shanty.

Target Triangle was another job where they resented a safety presence on their site, required by NYC law but not in their budget since they, used to working in PA, had not allowed for it. I could not write up my client, but I could complain to my boss about them.

But things were souring between me and my employer, too, probably because they were having to cut some corners to stay alive after the 2008 crash. I was told to basically "live with it" when the client pulled all sorts of questionable things. In some ways it was almost like being with the difficult NJ contractor all over again. But I had insurance inspectors and BEST Squad inspectors working with me, right? Wrong. The insurance inspector was adversarial. And the NYC Building Department sent some of the worst inspectors I had ever seen: power tripping, clueless, and useless.

Another fun fact: the job was in an unsafe neighborhood, with police cameras on the corners in an overt attempt to rein in crime. It didn't work; thieves broke the cameras and raided the jobsite for tools and materials on a regular basis, but only when the site was closed. I was grateful there was a security guard between the street and the parking area, but I still locked my car and left nothing valuable where it could be seen.

There was a college nearby, though, so the neighborhood at least had useful stores and inexpensive eateries. There was a deli across the street, next to the anime and manga store, that sold a hero (grinder, to those of you in the Midwest, sub sandwich, whatever you might call it) with four fried eggs, grilled onions, and four slices of cheese called a "Big Man." It made two meals for me.

And it was kinda fun, saying "I want a big man!" with a straight face when ordering. As far as sit-down eateries, and I liked those because I walked a lot on this site, there were several. At my favorite, a female cop who usually ate when I did and I got to talking. We were both older women, both dating, and had found that most men were intimidated by what we did for a living. Not that I had much time to go on dates while I was on this site: I worked 10-14 hours a day, plus my commute.

And all the time I was there, the client resented my presence. Target loved me; their rep was one of the sane voices on the site. But he got a nice warm office and I did not. My shanty was a way of the general contractor saying "go away." It was not insulated, nor was it really heated. No A/C in the summer, either.

I shrugged and worked from my nice warm or air-conditioned car, doing any paperwork with my laptop plugged into an inverter and my USB wireless modem. I printed things at home.

Other than the client's upper project management, the men on this site were great. The supers knew their stuff, and every trade had retained their best men after the 2008 crash. They were dedicated, hard working, and safe.

They did everything by the book when we had a crane delivery: PE drawings, permits, a skilled & licensed crane operator - even the required onsite inspection from NYC Cranes & Derricks. One of the idiot BEST Squad inspectors complained and took issue with all they did, and incorrectly assumed that we were not using flagmen when we were.

There were the correct sidewalk sheds around the entire site, too, that were beautifully maintained: lighting, housekeeping, signage, ramps, a red light for the FDNY standpipe location, proper permits. And yet, the insurance inspector tried his best to paint them as unsafe, unmaintained hellholes. I burned up a lot of digital ink proving him a liar.

Things were fine when I was there. I went on vacation, and came back to discover that they'd had a scaffold incident. A hanging scaffold they were moving off the site, which was only a few feet off the ground, fell on a young man and broke his arm. That was the only major injury on that site during my tenure, and it only happened because I was not there.

The one thing where the client broke the rules and had me tearing my hair out remained invisible to the inspectors. It was one of the most professionally dangerous situations in my career, and the only one that resulted in my getting thrown off a construction site by the client.

It started this way. It was early autumn, and safety managers all over the city were having the same conversation with their contractors: You, dear contractor, have to start the process for being allowed to have temporary heat on your site. It can take months, and you need to apply to the FDNY for a permit *now*. You can use electric heaters, but they won't keep things warm enough to let your men work or for things like plaster, concrete, paint, mortar, or caulk to dry correctly. Decide what kind of heat you want, and apply for that FDNY permit. You're going to need either propane or oil or kerosene heaters, and each choice also needs FDNY permits for storing the quantities of fuel you'll need to have on the site, and a safe place to store all the fuel.

My client at Target Triangle studiously ignored my warnings about applying for temporary heat permits. Then it got cold. Then they wanted it. And then they sent a grudging check into the FDNY, far too late. The local fire house came by to do a walk-through—they often do walk-throughs so they will know the layout of a new building or one under construction—and saw that they had temp heat set up with no permits. They got off with a warning since the client had at least had applied for permits and sent a check.

I later learned that the check and application had not actually been sent. I quietly went ballistic behind the scenes, and my boss pushed them until they at least sent the FDNY their check and their permit application. It was a better-late-than-never request to use the oil-fired heater already on site; it could handle the entire interior of the department store undergoing finishes, like a temporary boiler. It was approved. But since they did not want to pay for a fuel storage permit, too, they were restricted on how much fuel oil they were allowed to put in it. Half the 300-gallon tank was all they were allowed. So they hid a second full tank and only showed inspectors the half-full one.

It got worse. Brick was going up around the exterior of the building on scaffolds under tarps. The huge temporary boiler was not set up to heat anything outside the department store, nor could it; it was for the interior of the building only. So they brought in portable propane heaters. I just about had a cow, right there, since these were not only not authorized by the fire department, but the masons were doing things like working above the tanks without protecting them from falling bricks, and storing them incorrectly.

Right after I discovered this, but before I could solve it, the BEST Squad inspector showed up. It was a shell game, hiding these illegal heaters from him for this one inspection so I could save my client from himself. Had the inspector found them, he could have shut the job down for a minimum of two weeks, which would have made them miss the opening date for this Target, with its $1-million-a-day fines. Oh, and I would have lost my site safety manager's license, and my job.

The BEST Squad inspector somehow missed all the illegal propane heaters, but then thought he saw one. Remember how I described the inspectors at this site as clueless? He was about to write us up for having an illegal heater but he was pointing to a cart with an oxygen/acetylene cutting torch. Just so you know, they look about as alike as conga drum and a spare tire. *sigh*

So I showed the inspector what it really was, and he left without writing us up. And when the general contractor refused to see all of these temporary propane heaters as a problem, I went into the mason's trailer to complain. The mason, who was complicit, called the client and they threw me off the site in a huff.

I was never so glad to leave a place. Let whoever they sent after me risk their livelihood to let these contractors cut corners on safety. I, thank God, was out of there. And my employer still loved me.

Uptown Girl

I WAS SENT TO A BUNCH OF UPTOWN CONSTRUCTION SITES AFTER THIS, FILLING in for vacationing safety managers. The first was where they were building a new Courtyard Hotel on E. 92nd street. It was a great neighborhood to walk for exercise, and right next to an ASPCA shelter where I almost adopted a kitten. At this point it was mostly façade work, and the contractor as mainly working with articulated manlifts.

You've probably seen an articulated boom lift/snorkel lift/manlift; they are those motorized vehicles with a long arm and a work platform with a safety railing—a man basket—at the end of it. My main function was to make sure the men in those man baskets wore a fall protection harnesses and were properly tied off by clipping onto an anchor point within that basket. Should they not be tied off, all the vehicle had to do was hit a bump or the man basket snag on something, and they could be tossed out like tiddlywinks.

My main satisfaction was that I had the annoying John as my supervisor again for the first time in three years. He'd moved up to manager and was only doing site supervision for one of his overseers while they were on vacation. He was very trim and did competitive boxing up until he was over fifty. I was naturally chunky, and busy out of my mind being a single parent taking care of a dying mother while working. But John, with no sympathy, used to constantly taunt me about my weight, saying, "It's called safety and *health*. Safety and *health*. You need to get your act together." This still went on even after I managed to get equal pay and conquered more and more things than he thought I could never handle.

What John did not know was that I'd been on a low carb diet and lost four dress sizes. The stunned look on his face when he saw the new, slim me was priceless. All he said about the change was, "Well, it's about time." Despite my weight loss, he was the biggest loser since he lost his one last legitimate thing to criticize me about.

Confessions of a Female Safety Engineer

The next site they sent me to was a high rise under renovation on the upper west side, on Riverside Drive with a view of the Hudson. The project was at the edge of a very residential neighborhood full of brownstones; no stores or even a coffee cart. The usual site safety manager there was a hobby photographer and much beloved because he had an unusual strategy for getting people to be glad to see the safety rep instead of dreading him: he gave out prints of photos of the guys who worked on his site, as positive reinforcement when he caught them doing something right.

I did something similar. I had a repertoire of jokes that I would tell as a reward for good safety behavior. But the photos were tangible, and it was a great way to get the men to work with you.

On this site, which was right next to two towers built by Donald Trump, I head a story that made sense of something I'd run into years ago as an office temp. You see, there was a sprinkler contractor I worked for who wanted me to organize and catalog all of their reproducible "sepias" (a term left over from when blueprints were made by an older process). These prints on clear sheets of plastic would be valuable if they ever did an estimate on work on the same building, as they would be able to do a more accurate estimate. So I went through 30 years of these prints, physically organized them, and computerized them by address. Since my client was a subcontractor, I also noted who was the general contractor on each job. One construction company name kept coming up that I was not familiar with: HRH Construction. Who were they, and what had happened to them?

Once upon a time there were two side-by-side similar buildings being built by Donald Trump. He made it a contest between the general contractors who were in charge of each building. Whoever built their tower the fastest would get all of his business from now on. Let the games begin!

So they built, and they built. And the race was fairly even, too close to call, until one fateful concrete pour. The concrete supplier on one tower was different than on the other, and the concrete mix on one was acceptable. But the other concrete supplier left some of the expensive additives out of his batch of concrete, to save a little bit of money. This concrete dried incorrectly, and two whole floors had to be demolished and rebuilt. The company that had been shortchanged on its concrete additives fell behind in the race and never caught up. They lost the competition and lost their mainstay work with Trump. That losing contractor was HRH Construction.

Sometimes, New York could be cruel.

The project manager on this Upper West Side site had been a worker on one of the nextdoor Trump sites, all those years ago.

The biggest loser at this site was a homeless man who lived out in a shed on an abandoned dock out in the Hudson. The project was about to demolish that dock and put in a new one. He had to move on. So did I.

⚠

The third uptown job was a high-rise apartment building not too far from the uptown Courtyard Hotel. To get permission to build these apartments, the Owner also had to build a brand new public school a couple of lots down. So the project was at two locations: the school site (but not an SCA site, hooray!) and the high rise. And the high rise was on a corner, so there was a little confusion as about its address, especially considering that the new high rise was being built where there had originally been two smaller buildings, one on E 91st Street, and one on 1st Avenue.

Unfortunately, the building department was one of the places that was confused as to the property's address. So the inspectors would write up a construction safety violation at one address, and when it was fixed and/or the fine was paid by the contractor, the building department often did not credit the fix or the fine paid to the proper address.

The result was, when I got there, two three-inch-thick ring binders of violations that the contractor had taken care of, with almost none of the resolutions being credited to the contractor. The building department inspectors were convinced our clients were scofflaws that were not paying their fines and fixing things, even though they were; the fixes were being credited to the "wrong" addresses. So there were lots of very adversarial inspections where the inspectors found as many trivial "offenses" to write up as possible.

Now my boss had asked me to pay special attention to when the BEST Squad/NYC Department of Buildings inspectors showed up, and to call him with any over-the-top write ups. I had enough time to inspect and see that this was a very safe site indeed. This did not surprise me. Frankly, with them under a microscope they'd sort of have to be safe to survive. But that just made their persecution that much more unjust.

And that Friday, the building department inspectors came, looking for anything and everything to write up and punish our supposed scofflaw client. Their most absurd complaint was about the construction fence which was along a sidewalk shed, a covered walkway. They gave us a violation because the chain link fence above the plywood construction fence only went up eight feet, and materials were piled above that height that could fall on pedestrians.

Really? They were complaining about a stack of Styrofoam sheets. God forbid that any of that heavy and dangerous *Styrofoam* should fall on *anyone*. They might think they were being lightly smacked by a pillow.

I called my boss, assuring him that every single violation had been dealt with, but that the building department seemed to have three addresses for this site. Furthermore, the Department of Buildings website, which publishes the violations and the responses, showed them to be assigning the paid fines or fixes to different addresses than the ones the violations were written for. And then, as *la piece de resistance*, I informed him about the ticket they'd gotten for the threatening pile of Styrofoam. He thanked me with the air of a policeman who had just cracked a case.

I was working overtime that evening, again. I'd already picked up my car from the parking garage at dinner and was watching work on the sidewalk shed from my car. At about 8 PM I got a call on my cell phone from someone at the Mayor's office. I'm sure this official got my number from the Department of Buildings website, as I was registered as a alternate site safety manager for this site and my cell number was posted next to a picture of my site safety manager's license, but it was still rather startling.

"Yes, this is the site safety manager, Wendy Delmater. How can I help you?"

He apologized for calling so late. The official had to be working far past business hours, too. He asked me, "Could you tell me a little about how the Building Department is harassing the contractor at your site?"

So I told him, in detail. I explained the three-address problem, and suggested the official address of the building that was going to have replace them all, and that violations for construction issues the school be under that address for inspections until it was built. He occasionally stopped me to take notes and make sure he understood certain points, and specifically asked me about the "hazardous" Styrofoam we'd been written up for earlier today.

"Okay, I think I have the picture. Thank you for your help and your time." He hung up, and I just sat there and grinned. Thanks to my boss, the disorganized and overreaching NYC Department of Buildings was about to hear from the *Mayor's* office about this nonsense, and may God have mercy on their souls.

I came home to my family with yet another great work story to tell. We were all on pins and needles as to what would happen next!

On Monday, I informed our client about my little call from the mayor's office, and the poor beleaguered project manager was hopeful. The harassing visits from the DOB stopped happening, and the general contractor got an official letter of apology. Within a week, according to the DOB website all those supposedly unanswered violations were now cleared up and all of them referenced the one address I had suggested.

One of the things a safety manager does is protect the client, and that's what we did. It was immensely satisfying.

⚠️

The scenery at my next site was even more satisfying.

Just west of Central Park North in Manhattan, up Amsterdam Avenue, is one of the most beautiful church structures in the world, the huge Cathedral of St. John the Divine, its chapel, and its grounds – including the famous children's sculpture garden. My next project was within sight of this immense complex. The client was building a dormitory for students who studied at Columbia University's Teachers College, a few blocks to the west.

It was situated on Cathedral Parkway, also known as 110th Street. This site was in a vibrant neighborhood on the south edge of Harlem, with incredible soul food and all the benefits of being off a main line of the subway with a major tourist attraction. The nearby subway took me to my commuter rail, so I was free of the need for a car unless the boss was sending me to some other project after work. I had a nice client and a great crew to work with, and even the inspectors were reasonable. Would that all of my sites had been this pleasant!

Confessions of a Female Safety Engineer

I learned a new skill on this site, that of working with masons who—instead of using fixed scaffolds—used a long, hanging specialized swing-stage scaffold with a shed roof. It was open to the building in the front and would tie to each floor with no gap. The masons could work from this type of scaffold even when it was raining. Their crew was all very, very Irish.

Now I'd run into full crews of Irish masons before, most notably at Bellevue Hospital where they installed a sand-cushioned terrazzo stone floor in the huge lobby of the new outpatient clinic. But at this project, I learned that the Irish stone masons got those jobs through a network of football (soccer) clubs throughout NYC. I also learned where to get a good Irish breakfast in the City (*Saints & Sinners* pub on Roosevelt Avenue in Woodside, Queens) for my eggs and beans with Irish sausages, potatoes and brown bread. And I learned what *póg mo thóin* meant. Definitely nothing to say inside the cathedral across the street!

There was even a coffee bar nearby, with plush easy chairs where I could have a hot chocolate and warm up. I was sorry to leave this site when the vacationing safety manager came back. Tolkien once said that pleasant times don't make for great stories, but they certainly are nicer to live through.

DOWNTOWN BROOKLYN

THERE WAS A ONE-MONTH GAP UNTIL I WAS SLATED TO GO TO ANOTHER transit site. I had a little secret during this project, and the next one. I had finally met someone, someone I was serious about, and he lived out of state. I kept secret the fact that I was considering retiring at the age of 54, moving, and marrying this fellow.

But meanwhile, I was presented with a professional challenge. The residential high rise I was assigned to in Downtown Brooklyn was a reinforced concrete structure, with no structural steel. I'd never been on one of those projects, as they are some of the most challenging in the world. Making sure work went safely on one those dangerous structures was a real specialty, and my employer had (erroneously) thought I could not handle it. But like any dangerous work, if you follow procedures correctly, the hazards on such a project could be mitigated. I'd studied how, and now I was going to get my chance to manage one of these sites.

Concrete high rise construction is a fast-moving process that allows for a new floor of concrete to be poured every few days, with time to tie reinforcing rebar and build wooden forms around that rebar in between concrete pours. In the winter there is a really dangerous way of drying the concrete out that basically requires you to build an oven inside those floors, but it was spring: in warm weather the concrete just got chemical additives that made it dry faster. The fall protection issues were varied, and complex. Worse, there had been some recent incidents where passing vehicles and pedestrians were injured by things falling off this sort of construction. The Building Department was watching these sites with a hawk's eye, and jumped on any even seeming violation with heavy fines and threats of shutting the job down.

Another aspect of this dangerous work was that it used tower cranes that were bolted to the side of the building being erected and "jumped" levels when it needed to get taller. This sort of crane basically builds itself by lifting new sections hydraulically so workers can bolt them onto the top of the crane, while others bolt it to the new concrete structure every few floors. Two tower cranes had recently fallen in NYC, killing people and causing immense property damage, dominating the news. To say that such a site was under serious scrutiny by the building department would be the understatement of the year.

To add to the difficulty, the project manager for this client was another one of those "women don't belong in the field" types. At this point in my career, that just added a little spice to the whole situation. I'd show him that woman could do this. It was just work, work that you did with specialized knowledge and a bit of people skills; anyone with the correct skill base could do it!

This was a job I took the commuter rail to, and then walked a few blocks north past *Lindy's*, a restaurant made famous for its cheesecake in the stage play and movie, *Guys and Dolls*. The site was off Flatbush Avenue very close to the entrance to the Manhattan Bridge where the bridge soars over the trendy DUMBO neighborhood (Down Under Manhattan Bridge Overpass) before it crosses the East River and becomes Canal Street. I'd get very little chance to see the surrounding area, though.

I met the site management, in a finished part of the building off a loading dock, and was shown to my office. I shared this office with a young man who did nothing but check the embedded anchor point straps at the edges of the huge building. And there, I was in for my first shock. The Department of Buildings inspectors had concentrated their visits so much on the crane and potential for falling objects that the site safety manager that had just gone on vacation had not even had time to really do the required daily paperwork. His whole life had narrowed to that band of three floors at the top, and the crane, at the expense of his other duties. The challenge was not only to run the concrete pours, form stripping, rebar tying and crane properly, it was to get the neglected safety back on track for a very large project– including the site safety manager's daily log.

I did what I always do: read the floor plans, got site emergency numbers, then walked the building from the top to the basement, and all the perimeter spaces.

The hoist operator let me off on the 40th floor; I had to take job-made wooden ladders (which I also had to inspect) to the 43rd floor to start my walkthrough.

Wendy S. Delmater

The top floor was a jumbled mass of rebar work and wooden concrete form building. And I learned an interesting fact: since this work was so dangerous and no one wanted to do it, most of the crew up there were ex-cons. These men deserved to go home in one piece, too, but it took a little more conscious effort on my part to present myself as a tough-as-nails, no-nonsense woman they needed to respect. What worked the best was that I simply, honestly cared about them as people. They responded extremely well to that. There's a saying in safety management circles, that "They won't care how much you know until they know how much you care." That went double for this tough bunch of guys.

Once I was comfortable with the men's fall protection situation and the protections against falling objects, I checked the next two floors down, where concrete was drying or forms were being stripped. There were some emergency exit and lighting issues. Once I got below that floor there were endless fall protection guard rails along the edges of the building. I checked the openings where the crane bought in materials; even the overhang of those materials was regulated so that they would not pitch back out onto the street. And, finally, there were several of those mason's hanging swing scaffolds with a shed roof: I had to check the anchor points for the scaffolds and the guardrails on the sheds.

So many disciplines came into play. Temporary lighting. Standpipe. Elevator shaft protection. Crane anchor points. Hanging scaffolds. Concrete pump booster stations (which meant checking electrical safety and machine guarding).

This was all before I came down into the eight floors above ground level where they were starting to put the finishes in. And then there were the basements and the construction trades' shanties and the exterior of the site.

On the exterior they had an IDLH situation with incorrect storage of oxygen and acetylene tanks, so I got that fixed before even leaving the area. Then there was a construction yard, and I had to check everything from chocked pipes in storage to the backup alarms on heavy equipment, and flagging across the sidewalks. I checked the sidewalk sheds and pedestrian walkways for all sorts of things: lighting, housekeeping, standpipe red light and signage. Then I took my voluminous notes from my tour of the huge building and went to my office to whip them into a "fix these things" report.

One thing was certain, I told myself as my feet throbbed, *I'll probably not be walking this immense site twice in one day.* Or at least, one could hope not.

THE TOOTHLESS WONDER

SAFETY ENGINEERING MADE MY TECHNICAL-MINDED LEFT BRAIN HAPPY. BUT my creative right brain loved to write and edit. So when I discovered that this project manager (who did not think women could do my job, we'll call him Sal) was a budding writer, I tried that avenue to his heart with great success. Sal's memoir was good. I really enjoyed reading it, and my edits made it even better. Heck, it gave me something to read on the train, during my commute. By my second week there I was enthusiastically accepted as member of his management team. He even felt comfortable having me monitor the safety of "jumping" the tower crane over the weekends.

It was well that I'd settled into a better relationship with the man, because we needed it when the Building Department came to audit our site.

By this time the safety on the entire site was up to speed, except for one thing that bothered me. Just outside the orange debris netting on the safety railings, there were little bits of concrete rubble which were probably detritus of removing concrete forms. This rubble might conceivably be seen as a falling object hazard by the building department, so I wanted it gone. I got Sal to ask his crew to send someone up there to use a shop vac and clean off those ledges. It would take some time since there were over 40 floors with thousands of feet of safety railings, but that's what it needed. Sal got his labor foreman to do it. He spent all day on it and was only half done when he quit for the day.

Just then one of the building department's oldest, toughest, meanest inspectors showed up. This was a man who I'd never met before since he pretty much only looked at high rise concrete construction sites. I called Sal and asked him to get the labor foreman back up there with his shop vac, if he had not left yet. The foreman went back up and continued vacuuming.

I walked through this building for a second time today, my feet aching. I was on edge because this man missed *nothing*, and had a way of smiling at me that made me wonder if building department employees even had a dental plan. Sure enough, he complained of the concrete rubble outside the debris netting, but I was able to show him our foreman using a shop vac to take care of that. Everything else was ship-shape and regulation. Try as he might, the inspector could not find a single thing wrong. To give the man credit, he was pleasantly surprised. The inspector made a point of complimenting our well-run operation to the project manager before he left. I think you could have knocked Sal the project manager over with a feather. He's been terrified of being shut down, and instead his site was complimented? He called my supervisor to tell him what a great job I'd done.

My supervisor called me to pass on the compliment. He was rather in shock, too. "You went through an inspection with The Toothless Wonder and got no fines?" John was impressed.

Yes, I was working directly under my old nemesis supervisor John again, and he was utterly gobsmacked that I could handle a concrete high rise project with ease. He'd assumed such high-hazard jobsites would be too difficult for me to manage. He'd kept me off of these sorts of projects when my employer was incredibly short on those who could run them. So, with glowing praise that masked the enormous amount of crow he was eating, John promised me more work than I'd know what to do with.

I was now up to 80-hour weeks, if you included the commute. *More* work? God, no.

At this point I always slept in my clothes. I was so tired at night that when my cat would give herself a bath while leaning into my legs on the bed, I actually cried. Her movement kept me awake, but I was too tired to even shove her to the floor. I had no life outside of work. I'd had to give up my volunteering at my church's food bank and playing an instrument in their contemporary worship. I kept missing appointments with the woman I mentored. I was no longer writing. I had no social life. And my health was starting to crack under the strain.

When that man I'd met through the internet that seemed so right for me tried to talk me into moving out-of-state to live with him, I was already half in the bag. This job was killing me. I wanted out. I set up my vacation time to meet this fellow Brian in person. And the guy was really perfect for me: smart, responsible, fun, solvent, and cute.

He proposed. I said yes. And we set a wedding date without telling much of anyone. When I eventually told my employer, I'd give them a month's notice, but if they pushed me too hard, I swore-to-God I'd quit.

Multi-Station Edge Repair

One Friday I bade a fond farewell to the Brooklyn concrete high rise job, with Sal warmly insisting that I was welcome at his site any time and that I was one of the best Site Safety Managers he'd ever worked with. My employer, Consulting Inc., was going to send me to another long-term transit job next.

But first, there was my annual review that evening. I went into their new offices in Queens, which were so different than the makeshift office when the company started. I'd been hired when they had less than 30 people and now they had over 200 employees. They'd branched out into other areas of safety training, too. I saw several other women training to do my sort of work. The new facility was modern, spacious, and bustling. Knowing that I would be leaving the company soon, it felt like a farewell tour, and a glimpse at their great future built in part on my legacy.

My nemesis John was to do my annual review. He kept me waiting, and waiting. And waiting. I was penned in John's extremely boring waiting room for over two and a half unpaid hours. (Note to the younger generation, our cell phones were just flip phones back then, so when I say boring, I mean it!)

I had no doubt this long wait was a power-ploy on John's part. I was being put in my place. He was important, and I would just have to wait until he bothered to lower himself to see me.

Knowing I was going to give my notice soon made dealing with that little bit of pettiness ...sweet.

John finally called me into his office. It was spacious and impressive, and if that was what made him happy, fine with me. I bore him no ill will. I would be resigning, soon, and this delightful secret made me absolutely indifferent to all of the niggling little machinations that he threw at me during my review. Tsk - I hadn't been working toward getting a particular safety certification they wanted me to get. (You mean the one that would make me overqualified, unemployable except as a safety director? Told you I did not want that!) A grudging admission that I did all my paperwork well and always dressed professionally (well, duh.) A sad admission that this was all the raise they could afford this year (like that mattered.)

I think my utter indifference to anything he had to say unnerved John. No matter what buttons he tried to push, I gave him back blank stares, with no reactions. Fine, fine, whatever. Yawn. Are we done now? Good.

John gave me the parameters of the new project and the contact information. I was being assigned to a Transit job in the Bronx. Night and weekend work again, and maybe some daytime work elsewhere. I started tomorrow, Saturday.

Of course I did.

⚠

My new assignment was a subway station repair project. The main contract was to remove the worn concrete platform edge at a number of subway stations, and replace them with a fresh concrete platform edges that had a yellow embedded plate. This very nubby plastic plate would make blind people be able to find the edge with their canes, and was bright for the sighted to be more careful of the edge in the subterranean subway, too. It required more than a General Order, a GO, where the station would be closed during the work; the stations were closed for months and busses replaced them. Work went round the clock. All of the project was at various stations along the M line off Southern Boulevard in the Bronx, in a really lovely and safe Hispanic neighborhood called St Mary's. The area was full of bodegas (Hispanic delis), churches, lively residential neighborhoods, and various Central and South American cuisines. It was another job in the Bronx that I had to drive to, so I was paying heavy tolls again, but at least free parking was available.

The real dangers at this job were not the trains, but the clueless contractor, and some of my co-workers, who aided and abetted that cluelessness with some of their own.

One co-worker did something that was so insane he nearly lost his job. It was bad enough that someone got injured on his site in the Bronx, but the worker refused to go to a local, designated emergency care facility and instead headed for his own doctor, on Staten Island. Safety managers are required to stay on or near their jobs. This fellow broke that rule and followed the injured man to Staten Island to get an injury report, leaving the site uncovered for several hours. I discovered both the injury and the missing safety manager when I came in to take over for the next shift. I called my supervisor and let him know about the situation. It was a fiasco.

Then, there was the safety manager that did something so unacceptable that he actually *did* lose his job.

I had a co-worker, a safety manager we'll call Harold, who very often was sent to handle construction sites I had turned around from unsafe, to safe, to the point where he joked that he was also Wendy. Let me remind you, we safety managers pretty much work in isolation from each other. Unless we were on a round-the-clock project were we overlapped by a half hour to brief the next guy, we worked with our client but not each other. I only saw my co-workers at company-wide meetings, which were rare, or at the company Christmas party.

So I knew Harold, but I'd never really worked closely with him, and I'd never really worked with him onto a job, until recently.

It seems that our scheduler for Consulting Inc, who was always trying to get me to work more hours than I could handle, had done the same thing to Harold. And rather than fend her off and insisting on working reasonable hours, he'd given in, and was making up his sleep deficit by sleeping on many of his jobs.

I first discovered this when I filled in for Harold at a new apartment building project in Midtown while he was on vacation. When I did my usual thorough job of walking through a site and getting any problems fixed, I was called "finally, a real safety manager" by the PM on that job. Because I found out Harold had been openly sleeping on this job, and only woke up for inspectors.

And on my new project Harold handled one of the three full-time shifts, plus another full-time project. I'm sure the money was great for him, but I had a serious discussion with some of Consulting Inc.'s higher-ups about curtailing his hours, or anyone else who was tempted to work past his limits. There was no way in hell anyone could do a decent job when they were working over a hundred hours a week, even if they had no commute. They replied that Harold was younger than me, and if he thought he could handle that many hours they'd let him.

Confessions of a Female Safety Engineer

As a result, I ended up with Harold on my site, sleepwalking on the job and allowing an oxy/acetylene set up underground, in the subway station we were repairing.

Please allow me a brief digression into why having oxygen and acetylene tanks in a subway was against NYC Transit regulations. Remember that burning acetylene tank that melted through several floors of structural steel on my first big safety job? The one where we had to evacuate the site because the oxygen tank next to it might explode? Try imagining that happening in a subway tunnel, with buildings above it, on a busy street, where an explosion could collapse the subway tunnel and bring down all or part of an adjacent building.

There were alternatives. Contractors cordially detested MAPP gas, because it did not have much power to cut metal, but at least those tanks were allowed underground as that was a less dangerous fuel gas. The other thing you could do was have the oxygen and acetylene tanks up on the sidewalk level and run the hoses down through the subway ventilation grids. That meant paying for someone to keep an eye on the fuel gas tanks up there with but it was usually the best alternative.

There was no good reason to have an oxygen and acetylene set up down there in the subway. And yet Harold, "sleeping with his eyes open" to quote the transit safety inspector who found this, allowed an oxygen/acetylene cart right in front of him on the station platform. Harold had almost ten years of experience with Transit. He knew better. He was thrown off that project, and banned from ever working with Transit again.

And thanks to Harold, from that point on until the end of my work on that project I was in a struggle to not have my employer banned from all NYC Transit work too, now and forever.

The struggle came to a head on the next station we did. I mentioned the contractor was clueless, but that was inexperience in working in a Transit environment. It was his first Transit job. Harold should have warned him about things like not bringing oxygen and acetylene tanks into a subway tunnel. Now it was my job to warn this client about anything else that might be different about working with Transit than other types of construction. And like my employer, after the illegal fuel gas tanks were found in that station the contractor was on probation. One more mistake and he was out. Unlike my employer, the man who ran this contracting company had no other work. Losing this job would ruin him.

Wendy S. Delmater

The crisis happened when we had a transit safety supervisor glued to our site for a good 18 hours, sleeping in his trailer as needed, tasked with getting rid of both the contractor and my company if he could. But remember my policy about making friends with the inspectors? This guy was a friend of mine. As long as my client did not screw up during that 18 hours, we'd pass and there would be no more said about it.

I napped in my car while one of my company supervisors covered for me, but he was called away on an emergency. My friend the transit safety supervisor saw me back on the job, far too soon, and so did his boss. His boss wanted him to write us up for me working too many hours. But after the transit boss left, I pointed out that my friend the Transit safety guy was working the same hours that I was, so that would not fly in court. He agreed, and we both got a good ironic laugh. We were exhausted.

At the end of the 18-hour ordeal, the president of the client company literally hugged me and almost cried. I'd not only saved his company, but saved his house since it was the surety on his bond if the company failed. He was a nice fellow, trying to do the right thing, and I was glad to help him.

But it was time to get off this merry go round. I called the owner of Consulting Inc. and tendered my resignation.

Normally people give two week's notice. I gave him a month, since I knew I would be hard to replace and he was short-staffed. But I was ready to quit right that second if necessary. And my condition for staying on that month was that I would do no more overtime.

⚠️

From what I heard my giving my notice cause quite a stir at company headquarters. One of the other supervisors told me that my boss broke the news about my leaving to a management meeting the next day.

"Wendy's leaving us." he said.

"Who got her?" someone wanted to know. The assumption was that I had gone to work for some other company.

"Nobody. It's personal. She's leaving the business."

They were stunned.

Hotels, Art, and
the Meatpacking District

SINCE I WAS LEAVING THE COMPANY AND INSISTED ON NO MORE OVERTIME, they took me off the Transit job. The first few eight-hour days instead of 14-hour days felt like working part time. I could visit a florist, order a wedding cake, try on shoes, or go to a fitting for the wedding dress that a seamstress was altering for me.

And during my month's notice I was sent to three very mod projects, mod as in the old Mod Squad TV show. Everything old was new again, it seemed.

The first was a 60's-inspired building on West 28th Street, in a sea of *avant-garde* art galleries. I had ample time on breaks to walk this quiet neighborhood of exhibits. As for the project, other than me watching some of the work from a collapsible chair on a pile of sand they were feeding into mortar mixer and declaring it "as close to a beach as I will get this year," the less said about that place the better. Short version, the contractor was doing the foundation-only, pinned all his hopes on getting the contract for the structure above it, and lost. Very sad.

What was nice about that area was something called The High Line: a long, slim park that they were building on an abandoned overheard railway el. I really wish I could have worked on that project. It looked fascinating.

The second mod project I worked on during this period was a Euro-modern hotel back near the Essex & Delancey stations. That stint only lasted a week, but it was one of the funkiest weeks I had ever experienced. Fake-furry end tables, shag carpets, and retro 60s furniture and fixtures dominated the rooms, and some of the halls had neon-enhancing black lights. The concierge there wore—I kid you not—white go-go boots. My work was mainly in the atrium they were building in the back of the lobby, in the basements, and on the roof, but I had to check any work they we finishing in some of the units.

Finally, they sent me somewhere less trippy but more elegant than the Euro-modern hotel. This was site further south along The High Line. It was a 70's-inspired hotel in Manhattan's Meatpacking District.

Confessions of a Female Safety Engineer

If you've never been to the Meatpacking District, let me give you a virtual tour. Imagine a row of über-high-end designer retailers like *Versace, Helmut Lang, Christian Louboutin,* and similar boutiques sharing the same streets as actual, working wholesale meat providers, with boxes of sausages and steaks on wheeled carts and dollies sharing the same sidewalks as wealthy, globe-trotting shoppers on their way to an exhibit at the Whitney Museum of Art, or for cocktails at the famous Brass Monkey. The juxtaposition is startling.

At first it looked ideal. I'd requested a project where I would only have to do 40-hour weeks. The first few days were eight-hour days.

Then they asked me to stay, for an operation that would be ongoing and require a site safety manager until at least 8 PM every night. I had a wedding to set up, and yet they had still sent me to a job that was going to routinely run into 12-hour days! My employer's scheduler knew this. She tried wheedling and pleading with me. Couldn't I stay, just this once? No, absolutely not. Make me stay and I will quit right now.

I made It crystal clear that I could afford to quit right now, and did not need them.

I had to threaten to quit several times during the month of notice I gave them. They kept trying to push me to do them "favors." It just made me more and more certain I'd done the right thing with my early retirement.

⚠

I limped down the aisle as a bride, my leg still bothering me from the removal of that benign tumor in my thigh. The wedding was small, as second marriage ceremonies tend to be. But the sixty people who came were all very, very good friends. Only one safety management friend came: Diane, the woman who'd quit working for my company years ago, when that impossible supervisor John had pushed her too far. We're still in contact. Like war veterans, it's really hard to get others to understand what we went through unless they'd been there.

I assumed I'd be able to find a job in my field South Carolina. But there were some challenges as far as that was concerned.

UP IN THE AIR

As soon as I moved to my new home, I joined the local chapter of the American Society of Safety Engineers, to network. But several things got in the way of a smooth transition to a new safety job in my new home state.

First of all, South Carolina does not use the Federal OSHA regulations. States are allowed to have an equivalent safety regulatory agency, and SC was under a state OSHA, which was slightly different. That in and of itself was not enough to entirely kill my chances, but there was another factor.

Remember when I was researching a possible career in safety management and discovered there were three paths? Safety has three branches: Insurance, Industrial, and Construction. South Carolina does a lot of manufacturing. Almost all of the safety management work in SC was in the Industrial branch. And the industrial employers thought my safety experience did not apply, which I thought was kind of ridiculous. Analogy: Construction safety was insanely hard, like I used to run an ER...and now they wondered if I could handle a plant where things did not move and personnel was controllable, which was more like a first aid station. Sheesh.

So I looked for a position in construction safety. But there was almost no construction going on in the state, and the few employers who needed my skills were suspicious of my work experience all being in a state with labor unions. Then a construction firm called STV found my resume on the Monster resume website contacted me. It seemed that Boeing was building a huge new airplane manufacturing plant in Charleston, SC, and they needed a safety engineer as part of their bid. I filled a need for a critical position in STV Corporation's bid package to build that plant. I was listed as the senior safety professional on site, and supervisor to for four other safety managers. They named a six-figure salary, contingent on them being the winning bid, and submitted my resume as part of their management team if they got the job.

Turner got that work. It was an honor to be part of STV's bid package for a project of that size, though, even if that's all that happened. So I redid my resume to add that honor and was about to go out there and try for a new safety job, again.

But remember that limp? It got worse. The pain became excruciating. It was not merely left over discomfort from the tumor removal. I was diagnosed with a congenital hip malformation. The ball and socket in one of my hips were a third of the size they should be, with flat surfaces that had worn down over my 54 years.

Good thing for me that STV did not get that bid; I would have had to go out on temporary disability within months. My wonderful eldest son came up from Florida to help my stepdaughter and my new husband care for me during the ordeal. I could only imagine how impossible this temporary disability would have been if I still lived on my own back up in New York.

And while I was healing after the surgery my girlfriend Diane, who was still doing safety work for Turner in NY had an idea. Why not work for my ex boss, remotely?

So I offered to write safety plans and such for my former employer, at a 700-mile reserve. And despite the distance involved, some of these projects would end up being the wildest things I'd ever worked on.

REMOTE CONTROL

UNDERSTAND THAT WORKING FOR A SAFETY CONSULTING COMPANY FROM A distance was not as crazy an idea as you might think. Many companies and agencies wanted the entire safety program for large construction projects written out *in advance*, from the specifications and the schedule. And corporate safety plans needed to be submitted with subcontractor bids, or updated. So I called and asked if my ex boss had anything like that I could do. He did.

This started the remote phase of my safety career. My old employer took me on as an independent contractor. For my first project, they sent me information on a job that needed safety preplanned for New York City's DEP, their Department of Environmental Protection.

The Coney Island Wastewater Treatment Plant had an outflow that needed to be repaired as it emptied into Shellbank Creek. My job was to preplan all of the entire multi-million dollar job before it started. It was not just work that required my knowledge of OSHA and NYC safety law; there as a huge body of DEP rules that had to be followed. I was given a temporary access key to the DEP's intranet to make sure I had their latest regulations. The resulting Health And Safety Plan (HASP), which laid out micromanagement of the safety down to MSDS sheets and safety analyses of various tasks, also required me to do a lot of marine safety as there were soundings to be made of the deep creek bed. Oh, and I had to plan for sharks. Seriously. The challenges were unique.

First hurdle: I was given a PDF of an incomplete plan they wanted expanded. I bought a more powerful computer to run the only OCR program that would untangle the mess without me retyping it, and then reformatted and checked the entire document for software glitch typos.

I was not given any blueprints but did receive a number of sketches. So Google maps was my best friend since this job was all out-of doors. Need to plan a route to the ER? Google Maps. Need to choose a place for employees to gather and do a head count if the site was evacuated? Google maps.

Confessions of a Female Safety Engineer

The brackish deepwater "creek" involved was in a very populous area of Brooklyn, just north of Sheepshead Bay if you know the area, and next to a yacht club. The contractor was going to do pile-driving out on the water, to make a cofferdam (and area you could pump dry to work in). NYC insists that anything as noisy as a pile driver has to have a Noise Mitigation Plan written out and followed. Can you imagine trying to make a pile driver less loud? Not possible. I eventually recommended that they get approved hours from the local Community Board and just live with the noise.

When writing out a preplan for various construction tasks I always asked the superintendents how they intended to do the work, in sequence. Usually their way of going about things was sound, and my main role was to simply put what they were doing into "safety language" and thereby give them credit for the safe job they were planning on doing anyhow. Sometimes I had suggestions on ways it could be done more safety. Sometimes, like on this job, I was literally at sea. I had to do a lot of studying to even understand some of the processes and terms for marine construction. Luckily, I had friends in that part of the business, and I called them to give me a quick education for working offshore.

The final HASP was 73 pages long, with five huge appendices. It had everything from a map to the best local hospital emergency room, and forms they might need, a list of local emergency phone numbers, and all the safety training meetings they'd need for the project.

And the main thing I learned? Don't even mention the term "shark repellant" if you want talk about safety in marine construction. They'll laugh you to scorn, and you'll lose all credibility.

Yeah, I learned that one the hard way.

⚠

Another DEP job was "Improvements to Engines and Fuel Gas System" in Bay Ridge, Brooklyn. This was a huge project where they were putting in two backup alternative fuel systems at a DEP plant. It was even more involved than the Outflow project. For one thing, it was a renovation to an existing structure and those are always tricky. At least I had photos and blueprints to go with the specifications and the schedule this time! They sent pictures of the empty places they wanted to add the generators. And from the looks of the photos and years of experience, I ordered lead testing for certain areas before workers would install anything. A change order if they found any lead to abate was part of the plan.

Half of the work was the installation of two natural gas fueled generators, and the other half was the installation of some diesel generators. There was a lot of electrical safety and lockout/tagout to plan. Lockout/tagout is a system of making sure that machines do not start up when someone is working on them, by getting such machinery to a Zero Energy State, where everything from kinetic energy to electricity to gravity is taken into account. It got quite involved when I had to preplan the safe turnover to the owner, and startup, of these machines.

My final Health And Safety Plan, or HASP, for this project was 75 pages with sections on not just safety but requested section regarding Quality Assurance and disciplinary procedures. The Appendices A-F were so huge that I had to FedEx a DVD-R of them since they would not fit in a commercial email.

And, guess what? The client, the contractor, were thrilled with the quality of the work. But they complained that they had only wanted a HASP for the natural gas generator installations.

Well, they sent us the specs for both types of generators, and just told us to write a HASP for that. It took me five weeks. I and my ex-boss insisted on getting paid for them both, and they ponied up.

It was not our fault they never told us that half of my work on that dratted thing was unnecessary.

⚠

Another remote job was to preplan safety for a school in Staten Island, which required a lot of preplanning of trenching. This was, of course, an SCA job and I knew that sort of work quite well. I could almost write these sorts of safety programs with my eyes shut.

The remote work was intermittent, though, and then each one was a rush job. There was a series of jobs for The Department of Design and Construction, better known as the DD+C. You might have read about the DD+C as the lead agency that took over for NYC's Office of Emergency Management when that office went down with the towers on 9/11. Well, DD+C handles a lot of small jobs for the city, such as drug rehab offices and medical clinics. I preplanned the safety for several of these projects, and they appreciated my work.

I also preplanned safety for apartment building rehabilitations and had corporate safety plans to write.

I cannot say all of my remote clients liked my work. The worst one was a company that was building a new ambulance garage for the FDNY.

I kept asking their field engineer for answers to technical problems and he kept referring me to the site admin, who had no clue and was unaware of her cluelessness. It was the only time in my entire career that my old boss quit on one of my clients. They would not work with us. We gave up.

Instead, my ex boss set me up with the final, capping project of my career. It was fascinating. It was amazing. But our relationship soured beyond repair during this job.

⚠

Land in midtown Manhattan was scarce, but someone had engineered a way to put a skyscraper above the West Side Yard. This was a sunken train yard used by Amtrak, Metro North, and a little bit of freight – dead west of Penn Station and between 9th and 10th Avenues. The process involved bringing in a massive European machine that would basically build a heavy-duty suspension bridge over the yard; the building would go on top of that. Our client was that European firm; they were only responsible for this foundation, not the eventual skyscraper it would support. The work would be hand-in-hand with NY Transit and Amtrak. In other words, it was right up my alley. I poured over the schedule and blueprints with a fierce joy. *This*, I thought to myself, *looked like fun.*

At this time I was, as I mentioned, working as an independent contractor. Naturally, I wanted to work with other companies that were my old boss' competitors. He got wind of that and wanted to keep me working for him alone. So the terms of my work orders became more and more restrictive, until if I signed his latest contract for the West Side Yard safety management plan I'd be unable to work for anyone else for two years. I'd not even be able to flip burgers at Mickey D's. I ran the contract past a lawyer friend and his advice was to reject it utterly.

So, fascinating as the West Side Yard project was, when my old boss would not retract the offensive restrictions on my work orders, I told my ex boss I was fully retired.

In other words, I quit for good this time.

While I regretted not working remotely on the West Side Yard job I was happy; I could concentrate on my *violon d'Ingres*, my passion for writing and editing. My commute was now to my kitchen table to the coffee pot and back. Due to the sensitive details of some of these stories, I waited until a decade had passed to tell them, until they were parts of an irretrievable past.

Construction has changed since I left it. There are more robots like the demolition machine that took down the DEP water tower on my first NYC site. There is more modular construction, where things are built on the ground. I ran into a little of that: there were sheets of bricks assembled for MSKBIC's walls with lift points and put in place with a crane and ironworker—no scaffold. But the trend is toward modular construction of entire hospital or apartment or hotel rooms, assembled on the ground and fit together in the field.

Maker bots may take over even more of the assembly work. Smart buildings will become the new norm, with more data than you can shake a USB stick at being gathered from construction through digital as-built plans and operating manuals. Building Information Management software is replacing racks of blueprints that need updated with the latest changes. The smartest buildings will eventually have strain gages and leach detection built into inspection wells... eventually into the walls and windows and concrete itself. The continuum of safety planning will merge with downstream risk management.

How will that change construction safety? It will mean those who do it for a living will need even more computer skills. But it won't remove preplanning or inspecting the job. It won't delete the need for common sense or people skills. The processes I used and saw may someday become relics, but the lessons remained.

It was time to write this story.

Postscript, or
"So, Aren't You Some Kind of Feminist?"

WHEN I CHOSE SAFETY MANAGEMENT AS A CAREER, MEN IN THE CONSTRUCTION industry often assumed that I was some sort of "hate men" feminist who went into the safety management field to prove some sort of political point. Far from it: I love men, and I raised three sons that I am very proud of.

But I'm all for equality. Let's call that "traditional feminism."

I believe traditional feminism is necessary so that women trapped in abusive marriages, or abandoned with small children like I was, have options. At the very least, the ability of women to own property, to vote, and to work in a field that pays a living wage are all precious things. There are many places in the world that do not afford women these choices. And even the most traditional of women need these rights so we can stand on our own two feet if we choose not to marry, or if our expectations of the more traditional pattern of wife/homemaker/mother gets shattered by divorce or illness.

One of the wisest things my father ever taught me was that even if I wanted that "white picket fence" of being a traditional wife and stay-at-home mother, I'd better have a skill so I could support myself if that didn't work out. Husbands die, or run off, lose themselves to drugs or alcohol, or get desperately ill...or a decent one might not be available at all. So my father taught me to always have a contingency plan.

What's odd is that I became an accidental feminist. Although most of the guys I worked with in my male-dominated field were supportive and great teammates, I encountered my share of misogyny, sexism, sexual harassment, unequal pay, and disrespect because some men automatically assumed I was unable to compete in a man's world. I touched on those issues in my story; I'm not going to repeat them here.

But I would like to close with two stories illustrative of what I found that did not work, and one story that sums up what did work for me.

Back on my first big safety job, the courthouse project, we had a subcontractor who handled the specialty locks for the few holding cells in the basements of the courthouses. She ran a WBE, a Women's Business Enterprise. If your company was a WBE or an MBE (Minority Business Enterprise) government projects gave your firm preferential treatment when bidding as they were trying to increase the number of women and minorities on their projects. All well and good.

But this woman was combative and somewhat obnoxious. She was new to the business and did not understand how all sorts of things worked, and she assumed that any roadblocks to her success were due to the fact that she was a woman and men were giving her a hard time.

My girlfriend Lori and I pulled her into my office and gave her one of the choicest dressing downs I've ever been involved in. *Stop it,* we told her, *just stop assuming that it's all about you being picked on because you're female. You're embarrassing us as women. The fact is you are being treated like anyone else but you have no freaking clue how things are done. What those men out there said to you was a normal, regular part of doing business.*

The moral of that story is that looking through everything as if the patriarchy is trying to keep you down is often self-defeating. Sometimes you need to shut up, listen and learn. It may be a case of misogyny, sure. But it might also be that you're being a dimwit and need to get your act together and learn how things work. Do your homework, keep your eyes open, take notes. Understand that anyone, male or female, needs to go through a learning curve and earn respect as they move up.

Assuming that all your problems are other people's fault will *guarantee* that you'll never learn anything. Try assuming that you're being treated like anyone else, at least until you know enough to judge.

In other words, if your ship is an ice breaker, don't try to break up rock. Not every obstacle is ice.

I assumed all of the men I worked with were innocent of misogyny or ill will (a unisex thing) until proven guilty. There's *power* in positive assumptions; people tend to want to live up to them. Use that power to your advantage.

I'd like to circle back to the Hammer Lady. Remember how she blackmailed that sexual harasser superintendent? Well, when having a friendly talk with her one day she told me she also was related to someone high in the EEOC who showed her how to sue various, previous employers. She was a very angry and bitter young woman, but more to the point she was a very negative. That's where assuming that everyone is not on your side leads. Your very negativity makes no friends, and lawsuits on your resume scare potential employers to death.

In other words, if your ship is an ice breaker, don't try to break up the dock and other ships. You'll need them.

So what's the story that encapsulates what you should do? Believe it or not, it happened on line inside a bank. I was on that line, talking to a friend about how I'd gotten a minor injury on the job. I'd stepped on a piece of plywood that was in a puddle, not realizing it was coated in form oil, something that makes concrete forms not stick to the concrete inside them when it's dry. The piece of plywood slipped out from under me like a banana peel, and I twisted my ankle. The person in front of me enthusiastically suggested I sue the company I worked for.

"Why?" I asked. "It was a minor injury, and I love what I do for a living."

"Wow," he replied. "You're so lucky."

"Huh?" How was I lucky?

"You're so lucky that you love what you do."

I just stared, my mouth a thin line. I knew I'd be unable to bridge the gap in his understanding in a brief encounter with him as a stranger.

You're so lucky. There were so many assumptions rolled up into that small sentence. But the one that rankled me the most was that he assumed, outright assumed, that I had not worked *damned hard* to get a job I loved, a career that I was passionate about.

I ran into this attitude over and over again in the field, too. Men in semiskilled positions would often say things to me like, "I wish I had your job." I'd ask why, and they'd invariably reply that 'all I did all day' was walk around and talk to people and not do anything. I must have 'known someone' to get such a cushy job.

My standard reply was to tell them that all they needed to do to get my job was work eight verifiable years on a major building, take a 40-hour course, and go through a criminal background check. I'd show them how if they were serious about it as there was a shortage of qualified people in my field, and the pay was great. But they were a little misinformed as to what the job meant they had to do.

Confessions of a Female Safety Engineer

Being a safety manager meant pretty much memorizing the OSHA standards, and keeping up with any changes, including court interpretations of contested OHSA fines. Being a safety manager meant pretty much memorizing the NYC building safety code, and keeping up with any updates. You needed to know how worker's comp worked, EPA regulations, how to read DOT permits, and how to motivate people who wished you'd go away.

And when anything went wrong and people got hurt or killed, it would all be your fault.

All of my walking around and talking to people was just me making sure that the pre-planning I'd done, the training I'd done, were working so that all those laws were followed, and making sure men knew I cared so they'd listen to me trying to save their lives.

But it was a wonderful job, a great career. Did they want to get more information?

Of the scores of men (and some women) I had this conversation with, only one was interested. I'll never forget that tall, slim young black man. He got that spark in his eye that reminded me of when I first found out you could do safety for a living. It called to him. He took down all the information and assured me he would call my boss about it.

The rest of them just wanted a do-nothing job and were disappointed when what I did sounded like real work, which would take even more effort to get, so they turned away.

If all you want, male or female, is to have some sort of boring drone work to pay the bills, then by all means tune me out. But if you're willing to work toward something, look at what you might love and aim high. Remember, when I started out I was an abandoned, scorned single parent who'd been given a bankruptcy and a foreclosure as my "lovely parting gifts." When I started temping I failed the file clerk test the first two times, but I asked them what I'd gotten wrong. I learned.

It may take courage to say "I'm going to work toward a particular career." But at the end of the day, you have to live with yourself.

Dare to dream. Then work out a plan to be whatever it is. That applies whether your male or female. You're human. And if you need it, I'm giving you permission to reach for the stars.

It's the only safe thing to do.

Glossary

ANSI – American National Standards Institute, a private non-profit organization that oversees the development of voluntary consensus standards for products, services, processes, systems, and personnel in the United States. These standards ensure that the characteristics and performance of products are consistent, that people use the same definitions and terms, and that products are tested the same way. They are mostly known for materials science standards.

ASSE – American Society of Safety Engineers, is a global organization of occupational safety and health (OSH) professional members who manage, supervise, research and consult on work-related OSH concerns in all industries, government and education. The Society's members use risk-based approaches to prevent workplace fatalities, injuries and illnesses.

Bodega – A Hispanic/Spanish/Latino mini-mart, with similar products to a deli or a 7-11, but usually smaller and more like a liquor store atmosphere. Commonly used term on the east coast, especially in the New York City region. The word comes from the Spanish word for "grocery store" - la bodega.

CM – Construction (project) Manager. A CM is a company that uses specialized, project management techniques to oversee the planning, design, and construction of a project, from its beginning to its end. It differs from a General Contractor in that the CM acts more as a fiduciary agent to the owner and remains responsible for almost all phases of the building process including bid solicitation, job management and accounting. There is generally a closer alliance between the CM and the owner than evident with the GC and owner.

CPM – short for "Critical Path Management." This is a computerized construction schedule that relates each activity on a job to the overall schedule. CPM allows continuous monitoring of the schedule to see if you will finish on time, by allowing project management to track critical activities. A CPM alerts project management when non-critical activities may be delayed beyond their total float time, thus creating a new critical path and delaying project completion.

DASNY - Dormitory Authority of the State of New York. A NY state agency that is responsible for financing and overseeing the building of state facilities, usually college buildings, courts, or hospitals which serve the public good of New York State.

DD+C – Department of Design & Control, a New York City agency that is the City's primary construction project manager. They build many of the civic facilities New Yorkers use every day. They provide communities with new or renovated structures such as firehouses, libraries, police precincts, courthouses, and senior centers.

DEP – The New York City Department of Environmental Protection (DEP) is the department of the government of New York City that manages the city's water supply. DEP is also responsible for managing the city's combined sewer system, both storm water runoff and sanitary waste, and they carry out federal Clean Water Act rules and regulations. They also handle hazardous materials emergencies and toxic site remediation in NYC, oversee asbestos monitoring and removal, enforce the city's air and noise codes, and manage citywide water conservation programs.

DOT –the New York City Department of Transportation. Responsible for permits for street construction. They are also in charge of maintenance of the city's streets, highways, bridges and sidewalks and the management of a municipal parking facilities.

EEOC –The U.S. Equal Employment Opportunity Commission, a federal agency that administers and enforces civil rights laws against workplace discrimination.

EPA – The EPA is a federal agency whose mission is to protect human and environmental health. The EPA regulates the manufacturing, processing, distribution and use of chemicals and other pollutants. In construction, their primary influence is on asbestos and lead remediation, and careful wastewater procedures that do not release pollutants in the environment.

FDNY – The New York City Fire Department, officially the Fire Department of the City of New York (FDNY), is a department of the government of New York City that provides fire protection, technical rescue, primary response to biological, chemical and radioactive hazards, and emergency medical services to NYC. These are the folks with the fire trucks and ambulances.

FRA – The Federal Railroad Administration makes and enforces rail safety regulations, administers railroad assistance programs, does research and development in support of improved railroad safety and national rail transportation policy, is in charge of the rehabilitation of Northeast Corridor rail passenger services, and seeks to consolidate government support of rail transportation activities.

GC –General Contractor. A GC is responsible for the day-to-day oversight of a construction site, management of vendors and trades, and the communication of information to all involved parties throughout the course of a building project. They have a permanent staff and usually get their work through competive bids.

Grey Collar – Grey-collar refers to employed people not classified as white- or blue collar. It is used to refer to occupations that incorporate some of the elements of both blue- and white-collar, and generally are in between the two categories in terms of income-earning capability.

Hammer drill - A hammer drill, also known as a "rotary hammer", "roto-drill" or "hammering drill", is a rotary drill with a hammering action. The hammering action provides a short, rapid hammer thrust to pulverize relatively brittle material and provide quicker drilling with less effort.

Confessions of a Female Safety Engineer

HASP – Acronym for Health And Safety Plan. A project's HASP is its formal safety plan.

IDLH – stands for Immediately Dangerous to Life and Health. Also known as an Imminent Danger situation.

Lockout/Tagout – a system of bringing a system to a zero energy state, so that you can safely work on or with equipment.

MRI – Magnetic resonance imaging (MRI) is a technique that uses a magnetic field and radio waves to create detailed images of the organs and tissues within your body. Most MRI machines are large, tube-shaped magnets. When you lie inside an MRI machine, the magnetic field temporarily realigns hydrogen atoms in your body.

MSDS – A Material Safety Data Sheet (MSDS) is a document that contains information on the potential health effects of exposure to chemicals, or other potentially dangerous substances, and on safe working procedures when handling chemical products. It also has information on firefighting and safe disposal.

MSKBAIC – Memorial Sloan Kettering Breast And Imaging Center.

MTA – The Metropolitan Transportation Authority (MTA) is responsible for public transportation in the state of New York, serving 12 counties in southeastern New York, along with two counties in southwestern Connecticut under contract to the Connecticut Department of Transportation, carrying over 11 million passengers on an average weekday system-wide, and over 800,000 vehicles on its seven toll bridges and two tunnels per weekday. In other words, they handle the commuter rails, busses, and tolls for NYC.

NEC – The National Electrical Code (NEC), or NFPA 70, is a regionally adoptable standard for the safe installation of electrical wiring and equipment in the United States. It is part of the National Fire Codes series published by the National Fire Protection Association (NFPA), a private trade association. Despite the use of the term "national", it is not a federal law.

NFPA – The National Fire Protection Association (NFPA) is a global nonprofit organization, a codes and standards organization. Their codes and standards are designed to minimize the risk and effects of fire by establishing criteria for building, processing, design, service, and installation around the world.

NYCT – The New York City Transit Authority (also known as NYCTA, or simply Transit) is a public authority in the state of New York that operates public transportation in New York City. Part of the Metropolitan Transportation Authority, the busiest and largest transit system in North America.

NYPD – The New York City Police Department (NYPD), officially the City of New York Police Department, is the largest and oldest municipal police force in the United States. It has primary responsibilities in law enforcement and investigation within the five boroughs of New York City.

OSHA – The Occupational Safety and Health Administration (OSHA) is an agency of the United States Department of Labor. OSHA's mission is to "assure safe and healthful working conditions for working men and women by setting and enforcing standards and by providing training, outreach, education and assistance".

OSHA Star Program – Star is the highest level of VPP, usually reserved for general industry since it has a long time baseline. It recognizes employers and employees for developing and implementing continuous improvement workplace safety and health management programs that result in injury/illness rates that are below the national averages for their industries.

Owner – in construction, the Owner is the entity you are building something for. For example, if a general contractor or construction management firm builds a Walmart store, Walmart would be the Owner.

Pink Collar Ghetto – is a term used to refer to jobs dominated by women. The term was coined in 1983 to describe the limits women have in furthering their careers, since the jobs are often dead-end, stressful and underpaid.

Confessions of a Female Safety Engineer

PM – In construction, this means Construction Project Manager, usually the head of the site management running a particular job. A construction Project Manager's typical job duties include creating budgets and timelines, negotiating change orders, delegating tasks to subcontractors, and collaborating with other professionals working to complete the project. Construction project managers ensure that all construction projects are completed on time and under budget.

Rotary Hammer – see hammer drill.

SCA – the New York City agency that builds schools, the School Construction Authority

UCONN – The University of Connecticut.

VOC – Volatile Organic Compounds (VOCs) are a large group of carbon-based chemicals that easily evaporate at room temperature. While most people can smell high levels of some VOCs, other VOCs have no odor. Odor does not indicate the level of risk from inhalation of this group of chemicals.

VPP – Voluntary Protection Program. An Occupational Safety and Health Administration initiative where OSHA partners business and federal agencies to make a safe work environment. A VPP encourages private industry to prevent workplace injuries and illnesses through hazard prevention and control, worksite analysis, training; and cooperation between management and workers. VPPs enlist worker involvement to achieve injury and illness rates that are below national Bureau of Labor Statistics averages for their respective industries. An OSHA VPP participant is not fined by OSHA, who has a non-adversarial relationship with the client company.

WPA – Works Progress Administration: the largest and most ambitious American New Deal agency, employing millions of unemployed people (mostly unskilled men) to carry out public works projects, including the construction of public buildings and roads.

ENDNOTES

i. Megatrends, by John Naisbitt, Grand Central Publishing (August 16, 1988)

ii. What Color Is Your Parachute? 2017: A Practical Manual for Job-Hunters and Career-Changers, by Richard N. Bolles (Ten Speed Press) August 16, 2016

About the Author

WENDY S. DELMATER is the long-time editor and publisher of the Hugo-nominated Abyss & Apex Magazine of Speculative Fiction, found at abyssapexzine.com. She is also the editor of The Best of Abyss & Apex Volume 1 and 2, and writes science fiction.

Ms. Delmater used her background in safety engineering to write practical (and hilarious) guides to finding lasting love after the age of 45--for men and women--in the BETTER DATING THROUGH ENGINEERING series.

She hails from Lexington SC, where she married her webmaster and is living happily ever after.

ALSO BY WENDY S. DELMATER

Better Dating Through Engineering
Better Dating through Engineering for Men
Plant a Garden Around Your Life
The Best of Abyss & Apex, Volume 1 (editor)
The Best of Abyss & Apex, Volume 2 (editor)

Find her author page at
https://www.amazon.com/Wendy-S.-Delmater/e/B01C0Y19F8

Printed in Great Britain
by Amazon

48015936R00149